SPIRIT
MESSENGER

HAY HOUSE TITLES OF RELATED INTEREST

Books

Adventures of a Psychic, by Sylvia Browne

After Life, by John Edward

Born Knowing, by John Holland

Contacting Your Spirit Guide,
by Sylvia Browne (book with CD)

Conversations with the Other Side, by Sylvia Browne

Crossing Over, by John Edward

Diary of a Psychic, by Sonia Choquette

The Lightworker's Way, by Doreen Virtue, Ph.D.

Mirrors of Time, by Brian L. Weiss, M.D. (book with CD)

Visionseeker, by Hank Wesselman, Ph.D.

Card Decks

Dream Cards, by Leon Nacson

Healing with the Angels Oracle Cards,
by Doreen Virtue, Ph.D.

Magical Mermaids and Dolphins Oracle Cards,
by Doreen Virtue, Ph.D.

Miracle Cards, by Marianne Williamson

The Oracle Tarot Cards, by Lucy Cavendish

Wisdom Cards, by Louise L. Hay

All of the above are available at your local
bookstore, or may be ordered by visiting:
Hay House USA: **www.hayhouse.com;**
Hay House Australia: **www.hayhouse.com.au;**
Hay House UK: **www.hayhouse.co.uk**
Hay House South Africa: **orders@psdprom.co.za**

SPIRIT
MESSENGER

THE REMARKABLE
STORY OF A
SEVENTH SON
OF A SEVENTH SON

Gordon Smith

Hay House, Inc.
Carlsbad, California
London • Sydney • Johannesburg
Vancouver • Hong Kong

Copyright © 2004 by Gordon Smith

Published and distributed in the United States by: Hay House, Inc., P.O. Box 5100, Carlsbad, CA 92018-5100 • *Phone:* (760) 431-7695 or (800) 654-5126 • *Fax:* (760) 431-6948 or (800) 650-5115 • www.hayhouse.com • **Published and distributed in Australia by:** Hay House Australia Ltd., 18/36 Ralph St., Alexandria NSW 2015 • *Phone:* 612-9669-4299 • *Fax:* 612-9669-4144 • www.hayhouse.com.au • **Published and distributed in the United Kingdom by:** Hay House UK, Ltd. • Unit 62, Canalot Studios • 222 Kensal Rd., London W10 5BN • *Phone:* 44-20-8962-1230 • *Fax:* 44-20-8962-1239 • www.hayhouse.co.uk • **Published and distributed in the Republic of South Africa by:** Hay House SA (Pty), Ltd., P.O. Box 990, Witkoppen 2068 • *Phone/Fax:* 2711-7012233 • orders@psdprom.co.za • **Distributed in Canada by:** Raincoast • 9050 Shaughnessy St., Vancouver, B.C. V6P 6E5 • *Phone:* (604) 323-7100 • *Fax:* (604) 323-2600

Editorial supervision: Jill Kramer   *Design:* Tricia Breidenthal

Library of Congress Cataloging-in-Publication Data

Smith, Gordon, 1962-
    Spirit messenger : the remarkable story of a seventh son of a seventh son / Gordon Smith.
        p. cm.
    ISBN 1-4019-0269-3 (tradepaper)
    1. Smith, Gordon, 1962- 2. Mediums—Scotland—Biography. I. Title.
    BF1283.S616A3 2004
    133.9'1'092—dc21

                            2003007481

ISBN 1-4019-0269-3

07 06 05 04   5 4 3 2
1st printing, January 2004
2nd printing, February 2004

Printed in the United States of America

*This book is dedicated to
two of my greatest teachers in life,
Jean Primrose and Albert Best,
both of whom gave selflessly
in order to help others.*

CONTENTS

FOREWORD

As a psychical researcher, it has been my good fortune over the years to have known many mediums. Some I have not only watched demonstrating on Spiritualist platforms, but also had sittings with. Others I have worked with in PRISM (Psychical Research Involving Selected Mediums), the organization set up to bring mediums and psychical researchers together in order to study and evaluate mediumistic phenomena. Some, I am happy to say, I regard as good friends of mine.

Gordon Smith is one of those friends, which is one of the reasons I was delighted to be asked to write this Foreword. *Spirit Messenger* was an enjoyable book to read. It made me laugh out loud in places where [Gordon's] sense of modesty and self-deprecating humor push him into deflating any budding feelings that he's in any way special.

But he *is* special. Gordon Smith is a medium—a person who, in every other way, leads a normal life, working as a hairdresser. He demonstrates again and again his ability to receive information he simply could not have obtained through the use of the five senses. This is precise, detailed information, startlingly relevant to the recipient, conveyed either at a meeting place or during a private sitting.

Apart from Spiritualists and psychical researchers, the public knows little about mediums. In films, TV, and books, people are invariably presented with grossly distorted caricatures of mediums. In Noel Coward's *Blithe Spirit,* Madame Arcati is a figure of fun, although, in due course, Charles, the skeptical husband, is shocked to find that she is genuine after all.

The skeptics, especially if they have never studied mediums, easily explain it all away. Any ostensible physical phenomena are due, they say, to sleight of hand, misdirection of attention, or the practiced use of ingeniously fabricated or carefully concealed apparatus. As for the mental mediums, skeptics claim they produce their effects by a mixture of swift adjustment of a generalized statement, cold reading, and careful attention to the body language and verbal responses given by the eager-to-be-convinced recipient.

I have no doubt that in many places throughout the world there exist fake psychics or people who have genuinely misled themselves into believing they have psychic ability. Many of the former are tricksters of a particularly nasty kind, greedily leeching money from people who have lost family members or friends, people anxious to be convinced that death is not the end and that they can find evidence that their loved ones still exist. Such frauds deserve exposure not only because they prey on an extremely vulnerable section of the community, but also because of the bad name they give to genuine mediums.

Where I and the skeptic who dismisses all ostensible paranormal abilities part company is that over the years I have become convinced by the sheer weight of evidence that genuine mediums exist. Some I have met and studied; others I regret never having known. I had the privilege, for example, of knowing for many years the Glasgow medium Albert Best. There is no way the accurate information he gave a friend of mine and me could have been obtained in any normal manner.

Among the mediums who were before my time were Leonore Piper, Gladys Osborne Leonard, Mrs. Willett, Geraldine Cummins, and Eileen Garrett, to name but a few. Over the decades, some of the most intelligent, cautious, initially skeptical psychical researchers studied them;

people of the caliber of Dr. Richard Hodgson; Professor William James; Sir Oliver Lodge; Professor Charles Richet; and Gerald, Second Earl of Balfour.

What they found transformed their open-minded skepticism to a firm belief in the ability of at least some people's minds to operate outside time and space. Some, like Hodgson and Lodge, went further: They finally became convinced that the best explanation was that we survive the bodily change we call death, and under certain circumstances, can communicate with those left behind.

Most spiritualists and mediums believe that a medium—as the name implies—acts as an intermediary between those who have gone on, having left their dead bodies, and those still in this world. They believe that the medium demonstrating from a public platform in a church or hall, or giving a sitting to someone, is conveying information from Spirit to the relevant person to provide evidence that the loved one has survived. In hundreds of Spiritualist churches, mediums demonstrate throughout the United Kingdom (U.K.) and in other countries, and have been doing so for more than 150 years.

There is, of course, a wide spectrum of mediumistic ability, from marvelous to mediocre. It would appear that as with almost any other human activity, there are superstars, stars, and the barely luminous glowworms! Sometimes, as has been known for more than a century, the entire range of brightness can be shown by the same medium at different times.

Not only can mediums have their off days, but they can also be affected by the sitter [the person being read] from hell who sits back stubbornly, arms folded with a defiant look of utter disbelief on his face, plainly thinking, *Go on, astonish me!* Yet sometimes he *is* astonished when mediums of the caliber of Albert Best or Gordon Smith provide exact names, addresses, events, and descriptions sharply relevant to his life and the lives of those he has known.

I am not a Spiritualist, but a psychical researcher who, by the very nature of my scientific training, deals in probabilities. But what makes a medium? Are they born, do they develop or suddenly become mediums at some stage of their lives? Is it like football [what soccer is called in the U.K.], where it seems reasonable to suppose that superstars like George Best (a nephew of Albert Best) and Stanley Matthews are born naturally gifted in the quickness of their physical reactions, and subsequently, by long training and experience, perfect their abilities, honing the sharpness of their astonishing talent?

Many of the great mediums have shown signs of psychic ability from childhood. Such a child is fortunate to have parents who are familiar with these matters. More often in our Western society, parents react in a confused, dismayed, or even angry fashion, telling the child to stop fantasizing, forbidding them to tell such lies. Sometimes, however, the child's developing sensitivity is recognized by another medium so that help is given to come to terms with it or to develop the talent further.

The path leading to a career as a medium is by no means an easy one to follow. Often it has no signposts and the developing medium's life is frequently full of doubts and difficulties. Nevertheless, when one compares the accounts given by mediums, it is difficult to avoid the conclusion that among their diverse upbringings and experiences, there is a common theme. They are all aware of other facets of reality; they sense beyond the five senses; they are in touch with . . . what? By continuing to study mediums patiently, carefully, and comparatively, we have a chance to find out a means of exploring the deepest mysteries of human personality and spirituality.

I welcome this enjoyable and informative book, and thank Gordon for giving us this insight into the development of his own mediumship. Read it and journey with someone who has found himself a voyager on uncharted seas.

— **Archie E. Roy,** professor emeritus,
   University of Glasgow

❋   ❋

A Few Words from the Author

To all who read this book:

What I do means a lot to me, and for this reason I've tried to put this across as honestly as possible. People who come to seek my help have normally done so when their heart is breaking, or as on many occasions, they've exhausted every other avenue of help open to them. I truly hope that the accounts in this book may bring comfort and reassurance to you that there *is* life after death, not only for those who have passed away, but for the grieving hearts left behind.

Whenever I receive praise for my efforts, I often reply, "I myself am not so important, but what the spirit world allows me to do for others is."

— Best wishes,
Gordon Smith

❋ ❋

ACKNOWLEDGMENTS

I wish to express my grateful thanks to Linda Rowan for encouragement in getting started, Tony Ortzen for his editing skills, and Kathy Sorley for assisting on the original manuscript.

I also wish to thank Tricia Robertson, Dronma, Stella Blair, Rosalind Cattanach, Richard Rosin, Lee Bright, Christine Peebles, Mary Armour, Jim McManus, Martin Boyce, and Mrs. Preston, without whose contributions and assistance I could not have written this book.

Last—but certainly not least—love and thanks to my sons, Paul and Steven, for putting up with me!

✳ ✳

CHAPTER 1

THE AWAKENING

The day was Wednesday March 9, 1987, and I was 25 years old. It must have been just before 6.30 A.M. that I began to come out of my sleep. Somewhere between the sleep state and waking, a vision of a young man began to appear in front of me. My mind wasn't clear. I thought I was dreaming, but this dream was becoming more and more vivid. The young man was now fully visible to me. I recognized him as the brother of my co-worker and close friend Christine Peebles.

Christine and I had known each other since childhood. We were brought up in the same area, went to the same schools, and eventually worked together in a hairdressing salon in Glasgow, Scotland, in the United Kingdom (U.K.). Christine and her older brother, Brian, had just bought a flat together in the West End of Glasgow.

Both she and Brian seemed very happy with their new home. In fact, Christine appeared more content and positive about her future than she had in months. But she could never foresee the terrible and tragic events that were about to occur. . . .

A disturbing feeling went through my body that morning. I knew that something was very wrong and sat up in bed abruptly. With that, the vision of Brian seemed to

1

disappear from sight. He appeared to dissolve through the bedroom floor, yet my heart still began to race, even though I'd seen nothing disturbing about Brian's appearance. He just seemed to be standing in front of me.

Wearing blue jeans and a red checked shirt, he was smiling. His expression appeared to be very reassuring, but this terrible feeling of alarm stayed with me. I couldn't decide whether I was dreaming or if I'd actually seen someone standing in front of me.

Just then I had an urge to switch on the clock radio by my bedside. The time was showing 6:30 A.M. I flicked the switch and heard a man's voice booming out the local news: "A fire has swept through a West End flat in Glasgow!"

My heart was almost bursting out of my chest, and my ears were ringing very loudly. In my mind's eye, I caught a vision of two constables standing in front of me and heard myself saying, "It must be Christine." I just knew it must be her flat that had been burned out, and I feared that she was dead.

I never caught the end of the news, as there was a loud knock at my front door. I jumped from bed, threw on some clothes, and still half-dressed, opened the door to find two constables standing in front of me. I felt shock move through me like a bolt of lightning. My eyes must have been as wide as saucers. It was all I could do just to stare at them.

"Gordon Smith?" asked one.

"Yes," I replied.

"There's been an accident," he continued. "I've been asked to pass these keys on to you from a Miss Christine Peebles."

"Is she all right?" I asked.

"She's with a friend now," said the constable. "I'm afraid that's all I can say at the moment."

I took the keys from the constable and closed the door. The keys were for the hairdresser's salon, which Christine was due to open since it was my day off. It suddenly dawned on me that Christine must be safe, that she was not dead as I'd feared. *Oh, dear!* I thought. *It must be Brian.* Then the vision played over and over in my mind again. *Poor Christine!* Still, the constable hadn't said that anyone had died in the accident. Maybe I'd imagined all of this.

Sadly, it was not my imagination. By the time I reached the salon just before 9 A.M., the news came through that Brian had been killed in a tragic fire, and that his sister and a friend had been saved.

The strange experience that woke me kept playing over in my mind the whole day. I could still see Brian's face smiling happily at me and wondered why I'd had the vision of two policemen standing at my door just minutes before they arrived. Amid the sadness I was feeling for my friend, I started to replay all sorts of memories that I'd experienced in my childhood—memories I'd locked away in the deepest vaults of my consciousness.

In the days following Brian's death, a floodgate opened in my mind. It felt like a tidal wave of psychic phenomena that I'd suppressed since my early childhood. Now, it was playing back like a succession of old black-and-white movie clips. It seemed that Brian Peebles's passing had awakened a latent psychic ability in me, one I hadn't experienced since my teenage years.

After the funeral service, I asked Christine if there was anything I could do for her. She asked if I would take her to a Spiritualist church to see a medium. She was so insistent that I could hardly refuse, even though I felt that it would be wrong for her to attend something like this so soon after her brother's death.

I made some inquiries and found out that there was going to be a very good medium conducting a service at the Glasgow Association of Spiritualists in Somerset Place. So it was that Christine and I, together with Brian's fiancée, Fiona, attended this meeting.

The three of us sat together in the front row, with both ladies hoping to hear some news about Brian on the Other Side, although none of us knew what to expect. The medium, a woman in her 60s named Mary Duffy, was brought onto the platform. She had a very kind face, seemed educated, and spoke with a very polite Edinburgh accent. Mrs. Duffy didn't fit the image we'd conjured up of how a medium should look.

The meeting began with hymn singing and prayers like any ordinary church service, and it was all very pleasant. After the medium finished giving a talk on Spiritualism, she began her demonstration of clairvoyance. Almost immediately, she turned to our small party in the front row and addressed Christine and Fiona with great sympathy: "I would not have to be a medium to know that you just suffered a great loss." Both Christine and Fiona began to sob.

Mary was very reassuring and managed to relay a message from Christine's mother, who had passed on several years earlier. Mary continued by saying that Christine should try to seek out a medium called Albert Best when she felt that the time was right, for she believed he would be the one person who could help her through her grief.

She then turned to me and said, "Young man, I've never given a message like this from a public platform before, but I must tell you that your grandmother in the spirit world is telling me that you will one day stand on this very platform and give spirit communication to people as I'm doing now."

As Mary spoke these words, I noticed a very bright light that seemed to be emanating from her body—and with every word she uttered, the light became brighter. She then urged me to find a good development circle, try to be patient, and allow the spirit world to develop my gift of clairvoyance.

With this, she went on to her next contact. When the service was over, the three of us discussed the evening's events and agreed that it had all seemed positive. Christine was very eager to contact this man named Albert Best.

Unbelievable as it may seem, she didn't get that sitting (what I call a reading) with him until almost nine years later, but the results were quite amazing. She received a communication from Brian that was better than she could have imagined. I, on the other hand, was about to take my first step on a spiritual journey that would change my life completely.

✳   ✳

CHAPTER 2

A NATURAL GIFT

I suppose it was inevitable that I'd encounter Spiritualism at some point, for looking back over my childhood, there were so many occasions when I saw people from the spirit world or heard voices no one else was aware of.

The first time I remember such an incident I was about seven or eight and had just come through a bad bout of rheumatic fever. After my release from the hospital, I had to spend some time at home to build up my physical strength. It was during this period that I had my first clear spirit vision.

I was playing in our front garden at home by myself, since my brothers and friends had gone back to school after the lunch break. As I remember it, I walked out into the street on a bright, sunny day. Our road seemed to be deserted until, from the end, I could see a man walking toward me. As he approached me, I smiled. It was Ummy, a friend of my parents'.

No one in my family can remember how he got that nickname, but his visits were always greatly welcomed, especially by children. Not only our family, but all the youngsters on our street knew Ummy. He used to give us kids an old penny or a three-penny, depending on how he'd fared at the racetrack. Ummy spent most of his time around the racetracks of Scotland and worked for nearly all the bookies around the tracks at some time. He always visited us after having a good day at the races.

All the children used to mob him when he came off the number-four bus that ran through our street. He was the kind of man youngsters loved. Ummy would sing and tell us corny jokes, although I suspect he would have a few drinks before arriving!

Nevertheless, he was a harmless man and very kind. Ummy was the type of person who belonged to an older generation that found nothing untoward about a man giving pennies to children in the street. He always seemed to have time to play with the kids before going indoors to see my parents.

On this particular day, he was walking toward me from the far end of our street, singing something about "Dalbeth." I didn't know what this meant, but I joined with him and sang the words, "We will be buried in Dalbeth." As he got closer to me, Ummy smiled and just stood looking at me. I've never forgotten the expression of joy on his face. He looked so bright and happy.

As I moved toward him, something stopped me in my tracks. My feet were rooted to the ground. Ummy started to move backwards, waving at me as he went. I remember wanting to go with him, but I just couldn't move forward. Just before he disappeared out of sight, I heard him say good-bye.

As soon as he was gone, I ran back indoors to tell my mother, as I was very excited. My mother was standing at the kitchen sink—I think she was peeling potatoes or something. I grabbed her skirt and impatiently blurted out what had just occurred. She just stared at me, her eyes wide with disbelief. She shouted at me to stop telling lies. There was almost a look of fear on her face, which I couldn't understand.

"You couldn't have seen him!" she exclaimed. "It's all in your mind."

My happy feeling turned to sadness. I couldn't work out why she would say this to me. I was then told to go out and play and stop imagining things. It wasn't until sometime later that I learned that Ummy had died about a week or so earlier—and that he was buried in Dalbeth Cemetery in the East End of Glasgow! It's little wonder that my mother seemed so surprised by my claim of meeting him. I had no knowledge of his death, since my family considered me too young to be told.

After that experience, I became rather reluctant to tell adults about my encounters with spirit people. Nevertheless, on that particular occasion, I had no idea that I was talking to a spirit person, as Ummy had looked so solid, so real, to me.

Many people say that mediums cannot or should not predict the future. I would respond that whether or not mediums or psychics should predict future events is a matter of circumstance.

I'm sure that sometimes the spirit world feels that it's right to predict the outcome of a particular situation if this is helpful to the recipient in a time of need. Bear in mind that there are many occasions when it's not necessary to know the outcome of certain events in our lives, and finding out may even cause a disturbance. However, if they've gone through the proper development, mediums will learn to trust their spirit guides in these matters.

As a young boy, I had many precognitive experiences and visions. Mostly, these spontaneous predictions came about when I was daydreaming or playing. For example, one Sunday afternoon while I was fooling around with some toy cars, my mother and father came in, not noticing me behind the couch. They happened to be talking about Joan, one of my older sisters, who had gone out for the day with her then-boyfriend. He'd borrowed a car to take her for a drive.

I remember standing up from behind the couch where I'd been kneeling, and I interrupted my parents' conversation to tell them that my sister was in a police station in Carlisle—many miles from Glasgow—and that she would be home tomorrow. They both looked at me. Then, ignoring my interruption, they went back to their conversation. My sister hadn't been gone very long, so there was no way she could have been anywhere near Carlisle. Not only that, but my sister and her boyfriend were supposed to be driving locally, so it must have sounded as if this overly imaginative child was at it again.

However, later that evening after I'd bathed, I was sitting with the rest of the family in the living room when my father mentioned that he was concerned about Joan, as it had been sometime now since she'd gone out. My mother made light of this and said she thought Joan and her boyfriend would be back soon. Not long after that, I went to bed.

The following morning I got up for school, but nothing appeared to be wrong. What I didn't know was that sometime during the night, my parents had received a call from the police saying that Joan and her boyfriend were safe—and that they would be spending the night in the police station in Carlisle. They hadn't done anything wrong, but the car they were driving had broken down, and they couldn't get it repaired until the following day.

By the time I came home for lunch, my sister had returned safely. Nothing was ever said about my prediction, but when I walked into our living room that afternoon, everyone went quiet and just looked at me. For a moment I felt strange, then I asked for lunch and went about my day like any normal boy would.

✳

"Would you stop staring up at that ceiling!" my mother would often shout at me when I was a boy. "You have a really stupid look on your face when you do that. Now go out and play with the rest of the kids!" I don't know how many times in my young life my mother said this to me.

"What is it that you keep looking up at?" she would sometimes ask. I never used to answer, but would just get up and go outside. I never told her that I could see lights dancing around our ceiling or that Sarah was talking to me in my head.

Sarah Reilly Davis was my grandmother on my mother's side. She'd died in 1945 at the young age of 42, the same night that my mother and father were married. This left my mother to bring up her younger brothers and sisters. Just after their wedding, my father was drafted overseas as part of his Royal Navy service. This meant that my mother was left to raise her siblings without her new husband while still carrying the grief of having just lost her mother.

How hard that must have been, especially in those days when there was hardly anything to go around. Now, whenever I feel that life is getting me down, I try to remind myself how difficult my parents' lives have been, and I'm uplifted when I think of how they came through so many challenging situations.

It certainly makes me feel humble and proud to have parents as strong as Sam and Liz. Between them, they've helped so many people. They're both typical Glaswegians (natives of Glasgow), who feel much better about giving to others than taking for themselves. Many people have reason to thank them for their generosity, including myself, the youngest of their children.

My mother says that when I was born, the midwife who delivered me said that being the seventh child of the seventh child—the same as my father—would mean that I was going to be very gifted. Yet here I was being chastised for looking at spirit lights or hearing my grandmother's voice in my head. It was said that Sarah had been very psychic and used to read cups for people. If that were true, then why *wouldn't* she come back and talk to her psychic grandson?

When I was 11 years old, my parents took me to visit an old friend of theirs who lived in Blairgowrie, Perthshire. Ella, my mum's friend, invited us to stay for the weekend. It was during this trip that I had my first meeting with a Spiritualist medium.

On the second day, Ella's sister arrived. She was a small, stout lady, probably in her mid-60s. She had short gray hair, dark brown eyes, and spoke with a strong Perthshire accent. After some small talk between my parents and the two ladies, Ella asked me to sit in the kitchen, just off the living room. She gave me some paper and colored pens, told me I should draw for a while, and said she would come and fetch me in a short time. I couldn't settle down, though; I wanted to be with the grown-ups.

There seemed to be something going on. I suppose, like most children my age, I didn't like being left out. I was curious to know what was happening in the next room. After what felt like an eternity, I was allowed to join my parents and the two ladies. I could feel an excitement between the adults. My mother was saying she'd witnessed something quite amazing, while my father had a look of bewilderment on his face, although he just remained quiet. I didn't say anything but was dying to know what had gone on. It wasn't long before I found out.

Ella's sister, Sadie, asked my mother if she could try some healing with me. I had no idea what this meant or what she expected me to do. My mother agreed, and I was asked to sit on a chair in front of this lady. She told me to close my eyes and then put her hands on my shoulders.

Within a short period of time, I felt a slight vibration as though the chair I was sitting on was revolving. Then the healer called to her sister, saying, "Ella, come quickly! Feel this energy!" She sounded very excited. I wanted to open my eyes at this point but couldn't do so. Sadie repeated the same word over and over again: *clairvoyance*. Ella agreed that there was indeed a very strong feeling of clairvoyance around the boy.

Although my eyes were closed tight, I could hear everything clearly, including the word *clairvoyance* being repeated over and over again. I still sensed the vibration. In fact, it became even more intense. I felt myself starting to laugh. Although I tried to hold it in, the urge to giggle was getting stronger in me, even though I knew I shouldn't give in. I was trying so hard not to laugh out loud, but in my mind's eye I had a picture of both of these well-built women gyrating all around me. I was aware of my mother's presence . . . and knew she wasn't pleased with me!

Mum was whispering to Dad, who's partially deaf, something about my making a fool of these two ladies. "Look at him," she said. "I'll kill him when I get him home!"

My father was attempting to make out what she was saying, and replied in an even louder whisper, "What is it you're trying to say, Lizzie? I can't hear you."

"Keep your voice down, you silly little man!" she said.

"Your son is laughing under his breath at Sadie." She then turned to Ella and said, "He's always been a very nervous child." At this point, I burst out laughing.

After my mirth had subsided, Sadie spoke to me quietly and asked what I'd seen when my eyes were first closed. I gave a description of a lady I knew was Sarah, my grandmother, even though I'd never seen a picture of her in my life. (In fact, I didn't see a photograph of her until ten years after this event.) Then I gave descriptions of other people I saw. When I'd finished, Sadie said, "You have no idea how gifted this child is."

I looked at my mother, who didn't seem amused. She thought I'd made the whole thing up just to please Sadie. "Is that right?" she asked Sadie, who continued by saying, "By the time he reaches his late 20s, he'll become a clairvoyant, after which he shall travel the world and be known as one of the most famous mediums of his time. He shall also heal people in his life."

My mother interrupted this great spiel by saying, "Sammy, would you listen to that, eh? Our Gordon's going to be famous in some way!"

My father, who has always been a very quiet and patient man, replied, "Aye, Lizzie, that's good, eh."

After this great proclamation had been announced and things had settled down again, I overheard my parents' conversation about what had occurred before I entered the room. Sadie had apparently spoken to the spirit of my dad's late father and had given a perfect description of how he would have looked. She then predicted that my father, who wasn't working at the time because he'd developed rheumatoid arthritis in his joints, would restart his job at a certain time later in the year. Although Sadie may not have cured his condition, the pain did ease off enough to allow him to continue working at the same firm until his retirement some 20 years later. Sadie offered many other pieces of evidence, as well as predictions that all came true.

I was so excited that I was going to be famous as a great something-or-other—even though I'd already forgotten the word *clairvoyant*—that I couldn't wait to get home and tell everyone. Here was this lady telling me that it was all right to hear voices! I was filled with joy, probably because it seemed as if I'd been picked out and told I was going to be good at something. I started to imagine traveling around the world in the way she'd predicted.

The next day, as we went back to Glasgow by train, I asked my mother, "What was that word Sadie said I was going to be?"

"Listen, you," she admonished me, "you can just forget all that nonsense, do you hear? I don't want you to let that go to your head."

"But Mum—, " I protested.

"I do not want to hear another word about this!" she continued—and that was the end of that. My great fame was never to be mentioned again.

It seems strange to me that so many of my childhood memories have been buried away deep inside me for so long. But as I allowed myself to regress, I found that so often I was afraid to tell people about my psychic experiences since I was always being scolded for telling lies or being told that it was all in my imagination.

I was even told that it was "bad" to do such things. It's no wonder that I wanted to stop hearing and seeing spirit people, especially when I think about the reactions of the adults around me. However, now I can see that they were probably trying to protect me from something they simply didn't understand.

❄   ❄

CHAPTER 3

SPIRITUAL DEVELOPMENT

A month or so after the death of Brian Peebles, I began to visit all the Spiritualist churches I could find. Although every medium I encountered told me I should join a development circle, no one ever explained how I might do so. Many circles are held in mediums' homes, with entry by invitation only. After much searching, I found a group at the small Spiritualist church on Glasgow's West Princes Street.

It was run by Jean Primrose, a lady in her late 70s who had devoted most of her life to Spiritualism and who'd headed this church for almost 50 years. As well as being president, Jean was also a very gifted medium and healer. She called a spade a spade, never suffering fools gladly. Hers was what is known as an "open circle," with people coming and going from time to time, so I was welcomed into the Thursday-night group.

This became my spiritual classroom for the next six years. During that time, I learned to develop the spiritual gifts that had been with me since childhood. Not only was I taught to develop mediumship, but I was also encouraged to cultivate the healing gift that had been seen so many years before.

However, spiritual development is not only about healing or clairvoyance. It also opens up your mind and fosters self-awareness, which allows you to gain a greater understanding of your spiritual nature, that of other people, and indeed the nature of life itself.

The first night I sat in the circle, I was very apprehensive, since I had no idea what would happen. I remember thinking that I wanted to get up and leave, but that thought had no sooner occurred than Mrs. Primrose walked in. She was no more than 4'10" tall, but her presence seemed to fill the entire room. Everyone sat up straight, like schoolchildren jolted by the sudden appearance of their headmistress.

The room was about the size of a large sitting room. In recent years, the building had been let out as three separate properties, the church rooms on the ground floor, with two flats above. The room we occupied was to the front of the property, the largest of four that together made up the church. The other rooms were an office, a small library, and a kitchen/tea room, where people congregated after each service.

Here I was at my first circle, sitting in a group of about 40 people, chairs positioned around the walls. It was more of a square than a circle. Still, it seemed to serve the purpose. I sat near the front of the church, not too far from where Mrs. Primrose was conducting the session. Just behind me was a small wooden rostrum with a glass front, upon which sat a statue of praying hands. Hanging on the wall behind this was a large lithograph of Christ, which I found very calming.

Mrs. Primrose asked everyone to put their feet flat on the floor and sit comfortably, then began to sing, "The Lord Is My Shepherd." Soon, everyone joined in. For the first time, I felt a strong feeling of harmony as the voices blended together. This was followed by the Lord's Prayer, another hymn, and then the circle commenced.

"Close your eyes, relax, and listen to the music," Mrs. Primrose instructed. I was anxious to know if there were any spirits floating around the room. In the midst of my mental wanderings, the silence was broken by the sound of a man's voice, speaking in what sounded like an Indian accent. He said he was a teacher from a very high realm of the spirit world, and that he had come to teach us about compassion.

I couldn't keep my eyes closed any longer, and hoped that this evolved entity might be visible to the naked eye. But when I looked toward the far end of the church, where the voice was emanating from, all I could see was a short, stout gray-haired man in his 50s who was on his feet, eyes tightly shut, and speaking in what now sounded like a very exaggerated Asian accent.

At first, I did try to make sense of this so-called philosophy, but not too long into the supposedly spiritual dialogue, I noticed that the highly evolved one's Asian accent became padded with a Glaswegian dialect. He used phrases like, "We have come to help you, so we huv," or "Try tae look efter yur wee-ans better thin yur doin," and so on. The latter translates as something like, "Try to look after your children better than you are at the moment."

As if this wasn't bad enough, the Glasgow guru was then joined by a huge woman sitting opposite him purporting to channel an Asian female. She began her spiritual address with the words: "By the way," in what sounded like Chinese-restaurant English. I was on the verge of laughing out loud when thankfully Mrs. Primrose interrupted this crazy charade by asking both parties to sit down and be quiet. *Sanity at long last,* I thought.

It would appear that Mrs. Primrose didn't take this obvious play-acting too seriously. There are times when people's imaginations can run wild, especially in this type of situation. I also noticed that May, Mrs. Primrose's daughter, was very attuned concerning who was genuine or not, although I'm sure that the two individuals mentioned were not deliberately fraudulent, but just misguided or suffering from wishful thinking.

The rest of the evening went quite well, apart from these few dramatic outbursts of Glaswegian philosophy. I didn't experience any encounters with the spirit world on my first night, although several people did.

After the circle was brought to a close, most of the people gathered in the small tearoom, where they shared stories of their particular experiences. I listened intently. It would seem that while the "Asian floor show" was taking place, many of the more established sitters (people who are being read) were linking with their spirit guides and helpers while in a sort of meditative state. I think I failed to recognize the finer points of the circle the first night, but I was nevertheless intrigued by some of the stories shared by these people at the end of the evening.

If I was going to try to develop my spirituality, I would have to learn the dos and don'ts of Spiritualist circles. Spiritual development is, after all, a learning experience. It is therefore acceptable for apprentices to make mistakes. If I were to continue in this class, then I would have to be able to recognize the difference between my own imaginings and a natural ability to perceive spirit people.

In every training program in our lives, we make mistakes, and we learn from these errors. But if we can begin to laugh at our missteps, it makes learning so much easier. There's no such thing as right and wrong if you're willing to get something productive from a situation. Many of my greatest learning experiences came about through witnessing how *not* to do things. Let me highlight some of the more lighthearted moments on my journey.

A lady who sat in our circle for only one session confidently claimed that she had now spent enough time training and was now ready to become a medium of great importance. I made a comment that the lady in question must have considered herself a bit like Kodak film: If she were left for an hour or so in a darkened room, then she would indeed develop. I believe she had trouble with this concept due to underexposure!

Spirit Guides

If there's a problem with spirit guides, it's the way in which people interpret them. Never a night passed in our circle without someone claiming to have a guide of high order or notability. In my time in the circle, there were several people claiming to be channeling John the Baptist, Mother Teresa, the odd Gandhi here and there, and so many popes and bishops that you could barely count them. Oh, and even Jesus was purported to be coming through one man openly and a few more on the sly. Wouldn't you think that these people had done their bit for spirituality when they were on Earth?

I'll always remember the remark made by one of the women in the circle after a man in a so-called trance claimed that John the Baptist was speaking through him. When her friend asked if she'd like to be baptized by the "holy one," she replied, "I think I'll wait until he channels someone else. That big idiot he's channeling through now gives me the willies." Apparently, this same man claimed to have the Blessed Virgin in his cupboard at home. No wonder the success rate of healing at Lourdes has failed—Mary is locked in a pantry in Glasgow!

Some people get caught up with the idea of having important spirit guides. Sadly, this is the image many have of all mediums and Spiritualists. I do wish that they'd think for a moment before believing such nonsense. A little bit of common sense is all that's required.

During one of the monthly discussion groups that was held after our development circle, the man who was chairing that evening threw out a question to us, one that's often put to mediums: "Why are spirit guides either North American Indians or ancient Chinese masters?"

While most of the others searched for a deep and meaningful answer, I said, "Could it be that there's such a long waiting list for that type of position on the Other Side that that's as far as they got? I suppose people like us have no chance." Somehow, I don't really believe that's the answer!

If nothing else, I've developed a sense of humor. After all, I'm certain that those on the Other Side love nothing more than hearing us laugh. The ability to find humor in some of these situations was what allowed me and many others to carry on with our spiritual lessons. But aside from the humor, there were also times when spirit guides allowed us to feel some truly beautiful spiritual experiences—moments I'll always remember. Most of these memorable occasions are meaningful to me alone, so there's no point in sharing them with anyone else. Spiritual events seem to lose their importance when you share them with others; they can only truly be understood by the person they happen to.

As well as developing on my own, I witnessed some fine mediumship during this time, especially the trance gift of a very special teacher. One of the true qualities of any medium, no matter which field of mediumship they work in, is their humility. I consider myself fortunate to have been taught by such a medium. For the purpose of this book, I shall use only her first name, Laura.

This lady was indeed a trance medium, and a very genuine one at that. Whenever Laura allowed herself to be used as a channel, you could feel the very essence of the spirit people who spoke through her. Even though I've witnessed many trance sessions through Laura, I shall recount only one, which took place in the church after we finished our circle.

Laura seemed to drift off into trance, as she did very naturally. As we sat in this well-lit room, it was clear that something was happening. You can always tell when spirit friends are close, for the atmosphere in the room totally changes. The temperature drops, but not in a chilly way. It's as though the heat in the room is being used to fuel events about to take place. I'm never uncomfortable with this change. If anything, it's quite exciting.

We were all waiting to hear who would come through and speak to us that night. Usually, it would be one of Laura's guides, but on this occasion, a man's voice spoke. He sounded confused and afraid, and was asking if he could be left alone.

"Who are you?" I asked. The man told me his real name, but I will call him Mr. Brown.

"When did you die?" I continued.

"I'm not dead," he replied rather indignantly. *Oh,* I thought, *maybe he's calling from a nearby phone booth!*

"What do you mean, you haven't died?"

23

"I'm here in a hospital," he said.

"Which hospital?" I asked.

Mr. Brown told us the name of the hospital and also the ward number. All of this information, I remember thinking, could later be checked out, as it was a Glasgow hospital not too far from where we were. Mr. Brown went on to tell us that his body was in a comatose state, and that his wife and daughters were gathered around his bedside and were very upset.

He continued by saying that he could not wake up, and was so afraid to die because he didn't think he'd always been a good person. Mr. Brown added that he would much rather stay where he was, but hated to upset his family like this.

How very sad, I thought. *Here is this man lying there sensing his family's deep upset at his condition, and afraid to confront his fear of the afterlife because he believes there will be some heavy debt to pay.*

Mrs. Primrose spoke to the man, telling him that he had nothing to fear on the Other Side, and that he would be met by loved ones already there. She also told him that he mustn't allow his family to hang around his bedside too much longer, and he must consider letting go whenever he was able to. Mr. Brown seemed to pull back at this point. After a short period of time, Laura regained her full consciousness.

Anytime Laura went into a trance, there was never any fuss or bother. Some trance mediums go through great dramatic scenes, which I'm always highly suspect of. Laura gave us an account of the experience from her point of view, explaining that she felt herself floating out of her body, and that she was following a small light drifting in front of her.

The light became stronger and stronger, and at one point opened up before her like a pair of curtains. At this stage, Laura saw a man lying in a hospital bed beneath her. Three women were sitting around the bed, all very upset. Then she noticed that the man lying in the bed began to float up toward her. Laura remained there for a time just observing the scene, but was then drawn back toward us.

The following day, I checked to see if there was such a man in the hospital ward that had been mentioned. Believe it or not, there was. I wasn't able to obtain any information about his condition, since I wasn't a family member. But what an amazing experience!

The conclusion to this story came two days later when I got a call from one of the other people who sat with us that night asking me if I had the evening paper. I was then told to look at the death notices—and there it was. Mr. Brown had "gone home." The obituary said that he'd passed peacefully in a certain Glasgow hospital the previous evening, and that he would be much missed by his loving wife and devoted daughters.

Laura's mediumship has always been outstanding. The type of work that she does often seems unbelievable, yet it has always proved to be correct. I must say that I'm glad to have been taught by one so humble and understated in her work for the Other Side. So many times she's given herself to the spirit world so that others could be helped. Never does she accept praise or thanks for this. I'd like to think that all of the practicing mediums today could learn from her example.

Having witnessed the dos and don'ts of spiritual development and, of course, having made many mistakes, I soon learned that spiritual growth comes from within. If anything, the mystery of development is not about learning, but *unlearning*.

This may sound like a contradiction, but it's not. It's clear to me that when people first enter into the area of spiritual development, they're so hungry for knowledge that they practically devour everything on the subject, every book they can find on spiritual matters, every lecture or discussion they can attend. If there's a TV program on the topic, they'll be glued to it, no matter if the content is good or bad. Before long, they find that they've become very confused, totally sick, and spiritually bloated—they've had enough. This is what my Buddhist friend calls "spiritual shopping."

Like most people starting out on the spiritual path, I tended to overindulge. I remember reading about six books on spiritual and religious subjects at the same time. I was attending everything I could—clairvoyant demonstrations, discussions, healing groups. My head was dizzy with all of this, so I went to Mrs. Primrose and asked for help. She told me to stop trying to learn things in such a hurry. It was time to allow all that I'd swallowed to be digested.

I did so, and I must say that she was correct. All of a sudden, spiritual development became fun. Because I stopped *trying* to be a medium, the natural gift that was mine began to surface.

❋

I've learned so much from the teachers I've been fortunate enough to know in my life, such as Mrs. Primrose, Laura, Albert Best, and so many more. This isn't because they were teachers of great mysteries or secret knowledge, but more because of the people they were. Each of them had known so much adversity and tragedy in their lives, but somehow managed to overcome all these obstacles and evolve to become much stronger—while displaying great dignity.

It's now my understanding of spiritual development that lessons are laid out in front of us in our everyday lives, and we have to accept them with grace. A good teacher is one who doesn't tell you what to do, but steers you toward your lessons.

On many occasions, Mrs. Primrose told me that she knew I'd make certain mistakes during my development. When I asked her why she'd never warned me of them, she told me, "Son, I always wanted to, but these were lessons for *you* to learn. Who am I to deprive you of your experiences?"

This is how I recognize a good teacher—someone who says little . . . but knows much.

❋   ❋

CHAPTER 4

OUT ON A LIMB

The shift from development circle to platform medium (one who performs before an audience) is one that I shall never forget. It reminded me of when I was training as a hairdresser in college. While I was studying, I felt confident and eager to practice what I'd learned, until the time came to begin working in a real salon. At this point, it seemed that everything I'd been taught went right out of the window. I was totally "de-skilled"!

Becoming a medium was much the same, in that my confidence in the circle was such that I was able to stand up in front of everyone and give spirit messages without a problem. But when asked to appear before a packed church for a Sunday service, I was a nervous wreck.

Whenever people who feel they have a clairvoyant gift ask me how to become a medium, I always answer, "If the spirit world wants you to work for it, it will make sure that you're in the right place at the right time. The chance will never get past you." This was certainly true for me.

One Sunday night while driving to church, I became aware of an irritating feeling in my stomach. It was the same type of sensation that I got just before I had a psychic experience or premonition. This was then accompanied by a voice in my head telling me to prepare. *Prepare for what?* I wondered.

It all became clear when I reached the church. As I pulled up in my car, I noticed that Steve, the vice president; and Mima, the secretary, were both standing at the doorway looking quite anxious. When I approached them, Steve told me, "The medium hasn't arrived."

"Isn't there a medium in the house?" I asked, trying to make light of the situation.

"No, and what's more, Mrs. Primrose is at another church tonight," he replied.

There was about a minute to go before the service was due to start. It looked like we weren't going to have a guest medium . . . until Mima suggested that *I* go on.

"Me?!" I gasped, looking at the two of them in amazement.

"Well," Mima went on, "you always give good messages in the circle."

After some further protestations on my part, I finally agreed, in the hopes that the scheduled medium would turn up in time to save me.

Here I was, some four years or so after attending my first development circle, about to demonstrate my clairvoyant abilities in public! I can't begin to describe how nervous I was at that moment. As I walked onto the platform behind Steve and Mima, who were hosting and reading, respectively, I could feel my insides shaking like jelly.

During the introductions, the hymn singing, and the readings that preceded my work, I prayed. In fact, I prayed so hard that I thought my head was going to burst open. I made so many bargains with God that there was nothing left of my soul worth keeping. I even offered the ultimate bargain, promising, "Dear God, if You help me to get through this, I promise I'll give up smoking." (I wonder how many other mediums can claim that one?) Prayer—the last refuge of every doubter.

No more time for prayers, no more room for doubt, for I was introduced as that night's medium. The last thing that passed through my mind as I approached the podium was *Help!* But then something very strange happened. It was as if I were a lightbulb and had just been switched on. All the nervousness and trepidation I felt disappeared the moment I went "out on a limb." I relaxed enough to allow the spirit people to pass their messages through to their loved ones in the church.

I can't say that I remember too much about the information I gave people that night. I was just so relieved to get it over with, even though part of me was really enjoying it. The moment I was signaled to finish the session, I began to shake like a leaf on an autumn day. It felt as if all the nervousness I'd experienced before I began was waiting for me in my chair.

To my surprise, I'd done quite well, and people were congratulating me for my good work. One woman asked me if I'd lead a session at her church. *That's a bit much,* I thought. After all, I was still shell-shocked from the ordeal. I might have come through it unscathed, but I was still feeling raw from the initial trauma of being thrown on the platform as a complete novice.

Getting over this first hurdle of public mediumship did give me an enormous lift, though. I felt as if I'd walked across a tightrope with no net beneath me—one slip and I might never have found the courage to attempt it again. As it was, I could now afford to look over my shoulder and see the gap of doubt bridged.

Now I felt more trusting of the spirit friends who had impressed me all my life. My only experience speaking in public was reading the odd poem or passage in church. But when you're asked to demonstrate as a medium, you have no script whatsoever. You really do go out on a limb. All you have is trust—trust in a spirit world that you know exists and the trust of those who come to witness your gift. It's at this point, where trust of the medium and the need of the people become one, that spirit communication occurs.

Now I had the problem of telling Mrs. Primrose. I thought she would be upset, as she never allowed anyone on a platform before they were given her seal of approval.

"Well, it was bound to happen sooner or later," she said. "And besides, all the reports I heard have been very good. I just wish I'd been there to watch."

Afterwards, Mrs. Primrose told me that she'd always known I'd be a platform medium and that it was just as well she hadn't been in the church that night, otherwise I might have waited years to go onstage. But she suggested that I work with her for a while, with me taking half the services while she took the other half. This we did four times in succession—and after that I was on my own. At first, I worked only in our church, but it wasn't too long before I was asked to demonstrate in some of the others around Glasgow.

When I started out as a working medium, I was as nervous as I'd been on my first night. Each new church I visited inspired a fresh bout of nerves. I was a nervous wreck a week before I was due to appear.

Whenever I finished a service and people approached me to say how well I'd done or to thank me for a message I'd given them, I used to try to act quite cool and aloof, as if I'd been doing this for years. But really I must have looked like a frightened rabbit that had escaped from a snare, soaking with perspiration and shaking like a leaf, only too glad to have gotten it over with.

In the first year I did this work, only two spirit contacts stand out in my mind. Both are very different, but together they sum up my brand of mediumship.

The first happened in a small church not too far from Glasgow. I was working away quite well when my attention turned to an elderly lady sitting to my left, a pleasant-looking woman with a lovely smile. When I said, "Can I speak to you, dear?" she replied, "Oh, yes." I proceeded to inform her that her mother was with her. The communicator said her name was Cathy, that she had passed on in 1969, and was with Mr. Thompson.

"Oh, young man, that's so nice," said the delighted lady. "You see, Cathy is my mum, and Thompson was our family name. That'll be my dad she's with. Oh, lovely!"

Everything was going fine until up popped the husband. I relayed the message, "I also have a man here by the name of Joe, who says—"

I was right in the middle of my sentence when she screamed at me, "Well, you can just bloody well send him back to the snake pit he's crawled out of!"

"But, Madam—"

I couldn't get a word in by this point.

"If he thinks for one bloomin' minute that I have anything to say to him, he's up a bloody gum tree!" she added. On and on she went, continuing with, "The day that rat-bag died was the happiest of my life!"

At this point, I couldn't stop laughing, and was joined by the whole congregation who, it turned out, knew her story. Unfortunately, I did not. It seemed that this little lady had been given a very hard time by Joseph, her husband, when he was alive. Apparently, she celebrated when he died!

On previous occasions, other mediums had given this woman messages from her parents, and so on, but I was the first to allow Joseph the Terrible to contact her from the Other Side. He was only there to beg her forgiveness, but the choice belonged to the lady. And if she didn't want to accept his apology, that was up to her. Who was I to judge?

So back Joe jolly well scuttled to his realm of guilt and remorse.

After the service was over, the woman came up to me and apologized for her outburst in church, saying, "Do you know, son, I really couldn't stand that man. It wasn't until I got my first pair of glasses that I saw what I'd married, and he was vile. He was also very bad to me. I don't know if I'll ever forgive him, but at least he gave us all a laugh tonight. That's something, I suppose." I still get a chuckle when I share that story with people.

The second memorable message is in total contrast to the first, but it still managed to strike an emotional chord in the recipient's heart.

One Sunday afternoon, I was working in a Spiritualist church on the west coast of Scotland. Passing a message to an elderly gentleman from his dear wife in the spirit world, I became aware of a presence almost leaning against me. There seemed to be a real urgency with this soul, pressing me to move on to my next message. I had now built up a picture in my mind of the spirit friend waiting to communicate.

It was a middle-aged woman about medium height and build, with short brown hair. She made me feel a sense of great impatience. I sent a thought to her that she would have to wait, while at the same time speaking to the gentleman I was dealing with. The ability that mediums have to speak to someone and at the same time hold several conversations in their mind with spirit people is an art form in itself.

Eventually, I concluded the message at hand, much to the gentleman's satisfaction and his dear wife's annoyance. I then asked the spirit lady whom her message was for. Immediately, she drew my attention to a young lady at the back of the church.

"That is my daughter," she said. I could hear the voice so clearly in my head that it was as if she were actually inside me. Now it was up to me to trust this spirit lady and pass on her message as best I could.

"Young lady at the back of the hall, may I speak with you?" I asked.

"Yes," came the reply, rather quietly.

"There's a lady here who says that you're her daughter. Is that correct?"

"Yes."

This time she spoke with much more vigor. At this point, the message came pouring through.

"Your mother says her name is Sarah. She also says that she has only been over a short while, maybe nine or ten months. Is that correct?"

This information appeared to be right. Sarah prompted me further to say, "Tell Caroline I will be with her on the third of October, and also that her little girl will be fine."

I had to ask, "Is your name Caroline?"

"Yes, it is."

"Well, Sarah says that she will be with you on the third of October, some four months from now, and also that your little girl will be fine."

With this message delivered, the intensity that I was feeling from Sarah began to ease off. The last point she asked me to relay to her now very tearful daughter was that her father was with her in the spirit world. His name was William, and they would both be looking after their daughter from the Other Side.

The young lady came to me at the close of the service to thank me for the message she'd received. She told me that her mother, who had only been 44, had died ten months previously of breast cancer. Her father, William, had passed away five years earlier in a car accident.

My God, I thought, *what a loss for someone so young.* Caroline could not believe how real this all seemed. She had come along to see what a Spiritualist service was like, but in her heart hoped that her mother might communicate with her once the demonstration began.

Caroline then told me that she was due to have a baby in the month of November, and how she wished that her mother could be with her at this time. I said I was sure that she would be, then told her to keep in mind the date her mother had passed on to her.

As I looked at Caroline's face, I could tell she was happy. I felt as though I'd really helped someone that night. Caroline asked me when I would be serving this church in the future. I told her it wouldn't be until December. "I hope to see you then," she said. "Thanks again." And with that, she departed.

When I returned to the church later in the year, there to meet me at the door was Caroline, with her new baby in her arms. "I couldn't wait to see you," she said, her voice filled with excitement. "My mother was right, she was so right."

It took me a moment to comprehend what she was trying to tell me. "My daughter was born on the third of October," said Caroline. "She was premature by one month, but as Mum said, she's fine." What's more, baby Sarah was "named" (Spiritualism's alternative to baptism) at the Spiritualist church the previous week.

※

When you see people lifted out of despair because of something you've been allowed to do for them, it makes you feel humble, especially when it's someone so young, with so much life ahead of them. I can only hope that what I do as a medium will allow people to get on with their lives in a constructive and more positive way.

Mediumship really can help people to come through their grief with less pain than is normally experienced at such times. After all, our message is that there *is* life after death.

✻

As time went on, I found that my work as a medium had truly begun. More and more of my time would be devoted to this aspect of my life.

✻　✻

CHAPTER 5

WORKING MEDIUM

Working as a medium in the early days, I was eager to demonstrate wherever I was invited, so I traveled around all the small, local Spiritualist churches. I was so intense in those days. The whole business seemed to be dead serious—no pun intended!—but looking back, I can see the humor in so many situations.

One night while driving to a church in Wishaw, approximately 20 miles southeast of Glasgow, I suddenly realized that I was on the wrong motorway. Chrissie, the church president, was to meet me at a roundabout (a traffic circle) just off another road, at the Motherwell turn-off. But by the time I'd changed motorways and eventually found the agreed roundabout, Chrissie had gone, probably assuming that I wasn't coming.

Having arranged to be met, I hadn't thought to ask for the address. My only knowledge of this church was that the meetings were held in the local Scout hall until they were able to move into their new premises. A flash of inspiration hit my mind: I would go to the local police station and ask where the Scout hall was.

By now, I was running about ten minutes late—still time to do most of the service, I thought. After I managed to obtain directions from one of the locals, I drove to the police station, parked the car hurriedly, ran through the pouring rain, threw open the door, and said in a desperate voice, "I need to find the local Scout hall."

The desk sergeant took one look at me, standing in my long raincoat panting like some sort of raving pervert, and said in a suspicious tone, "Now why would that be, young man?" All of a sudden, it hit me what I must have looked like. How was I to explain to this policeman, who by now assumed that I was up to no good, that I was a medium and should be conducting a service for the Wishaw Spiritualist group?

As briefly as I could, I told him of my predicament. He gave a dry smile and said, "You'd think that with your being a medium and all, you'd be able to ask for divine guidance." But in spite of the unoriginal comment, he finally gave me directions, and I sped off thankfully.

When I arrived at the small wooden hall, I could see the shadows of the audience inside. It looked as if they had all just sat down in unison.

Thank God, I said to myself. *Chrissie must have known that I wouldn't let her down.* They hadn't actually started yet, so I hurried into the main room where everyone was assembled and said in my most apologetic voice, "I'm so sorry I'm late, but I started out on the wrong motorway."

The people looked somewhat surprised to see me. A man standing on a small stage turned to me and asked who I was.

"Gordon Smith," I replied, hoping this would mean something.

The man continued, "But why are you here?"

"I'm the medium," I began. Then a horrible feeling ran through me, for out of the corner of my eye, I could see a sign that read "JESUS SAVES ALL SINNERS." *Oh, dear,* I thought, *I've stumbled into a born-again Christian meeting!*

Before anyone could say another word, I was out of there, sprinting back to the car and heading for home.

What an ordeal! I was soaked, exasperated, and downright fed up. When I arrived home, I phoned Chrissie and told her of my plight. She laughed her head off because the hall I'd gone to had been the correct one about two weeks previously, but the born-again people had the Spiritualists thrown out.

I now look back at this farce with great delight, although I'm sure that if I'd hung around, I would have been thrown to the lions. This experience taught me two valuable lessons. The first is to always get proper directions when traveling to a church. The second is to never wear a raincoat when looking for a local Scout hut in a strange town. Good advice for any aspiring medium about to tour the church circuit for the first time. . . .

Working the small churches around Glasgow was the best apprenticeship any medium could wish for. The people in these churches were down-to-earth and straight to the point. On a few occasions, I was even sworn at. The truth sometimes hurts, but there's still no greater teacher. Some of my best work came from these humble little churches. God bless all who keep their doors forever open.

By now I was gaining quite a reputation as a competent medium around western Scotland, and offers were coming in for me to work farther afield. Not only that, but I had a mountain of requests for private sittings. Typical of me, I tried to do everything. Like a spiritual baby who'd just learned to walk, I insisted on trying to run.

It was now right for me to take some time for myself away from Spiritualist churches and mediumship of any description. This was the best thing I could have done, for somewhere in the last two years I'd lost all touch with reality. My entire life was in disarray. I'd been running all over the place trying to please everyone and had somehow forgotten about myself.

Sensitivity is the one aspect of mediumship that has to be tuned to perfection. It's a medium's sensitive nature that becomes enhanced in spiritual development; the danger is that it can encroach on everyday life if not properly controlled.

As my sensitivity began to heighten more and more, it became so important to learn to control this part of me, otherwise things would appear larger-than-life. Let me try to explain it like this: In daily life, things appear to be normal. You might look at your face in a mirror one day and notice a small pimple. When your sensitivity is heightened, that same small spot will appear to be a face full of acne. Everything in your life becomes exaggerated, and you begin to see molehills as mountains. It's very difficult to keep a balance between the spiritual and the material when your sensitivity first starts to expand.

Learning to switch off mediumship is essential when starting out, and so often I simply needed to touch earth. I've learned to ground myself by doing ordinary things, such as washing the car or straightening up at home, and so on. It's very important to normalize yourself.

Whenever things really become too much for me, I take myself off into the countryside and walk for miles, or sit by a waterfall or lake—anywhere I can find peace and stillness. Nowadays, I walk in the country as often as I can, and always feel replenished and relaxed after my visits to Mother Nature's garden.

✳

The year 1992 was coming to a close. I had now been in my development circle for more than five years, and for the last 18 months or so had served churches as a medium. I had taken one month away from the spirit world and felt good about myself. I did some soul-searching and realized that I had to learn to say no more often. From now on, I would let my spirit friends guide me to the churches I should serve and ask for their guidance on giving private sittings. This is a great system, provided that the medium keeps to it, but as soon as I started back, I was off again on the roller coaster.

In the coming year, I found that I had even more engagements for churches, while my diary was full to bursting with appointments for private sittings. It's the easiest thing in the world to decide to say no—until the phone rings!

One day while working in the hair salon, I received a telephone call from a distraught female. The lady was crying, saying that she had to speak to the medium Gordon Smith. I informed her that I was at work, but promised I'd call back if she left me a number.

Late that afternoon, I called and arranged to see her the following day, which I had off. I instructed her not to supply any information about her life or situation, something I always do when asked to give private sittings to strangers. After returning and settling down to watch some television, I drifted into a snooze.

Although not in a deep sleep, I began to dream, and saw a young man in his mid-20s. He was reasonably tall, with short blond hair. I witnessed this young man running as if he were late for something, but then for no apparent reason he fell down. This short dream played over several times in my mind until I began to stir from the dream state.

When I opened my eyes, I could see the same man standing beside me, only he was not all there. By this, I

43

mean he was visible only from the waist up. Then he communicated something without actually speaking: "Francis John." Then he was gone. For the rest of the night, I asked my spirit helpers who this young man was, but it seemed that the lines were down. I was given no reply and decided to put it down to experience.

The following morning I dressed, ate a light breakfast, and headed off early to sit for the very distraught lady of the previous day. When I finally reached the address I'd been given, I was greeted by a man in his mid-40s. He showed me into the living room, where I was introduced to Mrs. Preston, the lady I'd spoken to. She was also in her mid-40s; had shoulder-length dark, curly hair; and was very slim. There was a deep sadness in her brown eyes.

After a short introduction and a brief rundown of how a private sitting works, I got started. The very second that I took the lady's hand, I could hear the voice of a spirit gentleman clearly in my left ear.

"Mum, Mum, I'm here," he whispered.

As I passed this information to Mrs. Preston, she instantly began to cry. At this point, I closed my eyes and saw the face of the young man I'd seen the night before, who had uttered the name Francis John. Then something happened that I had never experienced previously: I could feel myself going into trance. Although I had been in a trance before, I'd never given a private sitting in this state. I will let Mrs. Preston tell the rest:

I had never had a sitting with a medium before. When Gordon entered my home, I was a bit taken aback by how young he was. I really expected someone older. However, once he spoke to me and settled my fears, I felt quite safe in his hands. Gordon took my hand and then mentioned the words,

"Mum, I'm here," after which he told me my son's proper name, Francis John, which is what he was christened, although he was known as Franky.

Gordon said at the outset of this sitting that he would not go into any funny trance states, although that is exactly what he did. When his eyes closed, he remained quiet for a while, and then a voice quite different from his own spoke through him.

I was told that my son was safe and that he did not feel a thing when he passed away. I was then told the exact date that he died, which was ten days before this, on the 18th. It then became clear that my son was influencing the voice that was speaking, as he said things in a way that only he could.

My heart began to fill with joy as this discourse continued. Franky had been married for just over a year when tragedy struck. His young widow's name was Christine. During this session he said, "Tell Chris to remember the Lake District." This is where they spent their honeymoon. He then sent his regards to the rest of his family, each by their first name.

The amount of information that came through to me was all relevant to the life of my son and to the life of my family. At the end of this session, Franky told me that if I ever wanted to see him, I should look for the brightest star in the sky. This is what I would say to him when as a child he would ask where his grandpa went after he died. I always said, "Look for the brightest star in the sky, Franky. That is where your grandpa is."

I don't know what prompted me to have a sitting with a medium, but what I do know is that I have spoken to my son in Heaven, and he sounded happy. I just want to thank Gordon so much for his *very special gift. I hope that God will take care of him so he may be able to bring comfort to others who have suffered as our family has.*

At the end of this experience, I learned that I'd been sitting for slightly more than an hour, even though it only seemed like seconds to me. When the story was relayed back to me, I was quite astonished. Mrs. Preston could not thank me enough, saying she felt that a great pain had been lifted from her, and that there was a lightness about her that she hadn't felt since hearing the terrible news about her son.

When I arrived home later that day, I still couldn't comprehend what had happened. The level of my sensitivity had indeed expanded so much that I could hardly believe it. When you sit for someone who genuinely requires proper contact with the spirit world, the guides and helpers on the Other Side pull out all the stops.

Even now I'll always find time to sit for someone whose heart is breaking with grief. In this particular case, there was so much unfinished business that I believe my spirit friends definitely inspired the sitting. The only thing about working at this level is that soon I found myself in constant demand. So much for saying no!

✻ ✻

CHAPTER 6

MAKING THE GRADE

It was January of 1995. The Glasgow Association of Spiritualists was about to celebrate its 130th anniversary. The celebration was to be headed by two mediums giving a double demonstration of clairvoyance. I was invited to share the platform with Albert Best.

The prospect left me with mixed feelings. On the one hand, I was filled with pride at the thought of working with such a highly revered clairvoyant as Albert. On the other hand, I was terrified, afraid I might not measure up to this great exponent of mediumship.

Before the service, we shared nervous small talk. Mr. Best, I imagine, was trying to work out why this medium, who was almost unknown to him, was invited to appear with him on such a special evening. He asked me where I'd worked around the world. Hesitantly, I mentioned a few of the bigger churches in which I'd demonstrated. I don't think he was impressed at all, as he'd appeared all over the world. "Everywhere except for Japan," he pointed out. "But you'll work there within the next five years." Of course, I took this throwaway prediction with a pinch of salt.

We walked out of the anteroom together to view a rather overcrowded church. About 250 people had squeezed into the church, which was about 20 more than it could really handle. Outside, another 50 or so had to be turned away. Every time it was advertised that Albert was to speak at a church, this was the typical scene. It had nothing to do with me. I felt like an opening act that goes on before the main attraction to warm up the crowd. However, as I completed my work, Albert walked forward to the microphone and announced, "What we've just witnessed is a young medium who has the potential to be an *excellent* medium."

Albert couldn't believe that I worked the way I did. Later, he told me, "I was getting sick of being told about all these so-called brilliant new mediums," those who, in his opinion, could speak well, but who imparted very general information to people. "It was good to see someone who could actually do the work properly," he added. This meant so much to me at the time, and still does.

Mediumship was Albert's life, and he was always completely sincere with people. He had no time for those who were playing games with this subject, and felt even more strongly about the way some Spiritualist organizations were training mediums. So from that night forward, he decided to take me under his wing. What a great honor indeed.

Albert Best taught me more about mediumship in two years than most mediums will learn in twenty. Like my previous teacher, he wasn't a great philosopher. No, it was more to do with his own life experience. His greatest attributes were humility and a complete lack of ego. Albert gave private sittings to some of the most famous people in the world, and yet he never at any time mentioned this fact.

I still have some of his photo albums. They contain hundreds of signed photographs of pop stars, famous actors, politicians, and royalty from every part of the globe, all thanking this honorable little Irishman for his kindness. If I ever asked about these individuals, Albert would simply say, "Oh, they're just people who need help like anyone else."

This is how mediums should conduct themselves. Today, if a celebrity has a sitting with a psychic, an account of the person's private life is normally splashed over the front pages of one of the daily newspapers. This is shortly followed up with a book about the medium's life. The ethics of spiritual mediumship should never allow any genuine clairvoyant to divulge the private information between themselves and their client for a quick buck.

People such as Albert Best and Mrs. Primrose were decent and down-to-earth. The only real instruction they gave was by example. And what made them so good was that they'd known great suffering in their lives. But more than that, they were both driven to prevent the suffering of any other being in this world. The true act of mediumship is born out of compassion.

I made a point of visiting Albert two or three days each week. Since he lived by himself, my friend Jim McManus or I spent time with him at his flat on the south side of Glasgow. Albert was very independent and always fussed when we offered to cut his hair or take him to the hospital for checkups. He insisted on trying to give us things. Of course, I would accept nothing from him. This always led to great battles between us.

Here was this poor old soul, near the end of his life— and a life in which he gave so much of his time to so many others and asked for nothing. I know for a fact that he appreciated the time we spent together. His pale blue eyes would light up whenever I entered his home. He was excited to hear all about my work in the churches, and just as keen to know the latest gossip.

At this point in his life, Albert's mobility was very poor. Indeed, the demonstration of clairvoyance we shared in January of that year was to be the last time he worked in Scotland.

Albert was eager for me to work in all the most reputable Spiritualist centers around the country. The fact that it was Albert who recommended another medium to work in these places made people within the Spiritualist movement take notice, as the great Mr. Best had never been known to promote another medium before.

This man certainly had an effect on my life, not only in the psychic field, but more important, on my whole attitude to life and the way I viewed other people. He made me feel much more responsible for those who sought comfort from my mediumship. Because of Albert, I would have to say that I truly developed a much deeper understanding of other human beings.

I can never emulate this supreme medium. Even to try would be wrong, but if I can fulfill the potential he saw in me, I know he will smile down on me from heaven.

The last time I shared a conversation with Albert, Jim and I had just had lunch with him in town. We drove back to Albert's new flat, which was part of a sheltered housing complex. The three of us were talking about a trip that I was soon to make to Yorkshire for a seminar on Spiritualism when someone knocked at Albert's door.

Jim answered the door to find a very refined lady wishing to speak with Mr. Best. Albert introduced her to both Jim and me. But the strange thing was that he announced us as two plainclothes policemen! Albert was such a practical joker that the pair of us went along with it. The lady seemed to be none the wiser. Within a few moments of our strange introduction, Jim and I departed to leave the lady to speak with him in private. On the way home, we discussed this bizarre episode, not fully understanding the intent behind it. But with Albert you just never knew.

The following day I headed off to my seminar in Yorkshire. While I was there, I had a strange feeling that something was wrong with Albert. I phoned him, only to be told that he was fine, and that I should not worry about him so much.

When I eventually did get home at the end of the week, Jim informed me that Albert was in the hospital, comatose. Immediately, I rushed to see him. For the next ten days, his condition remained the same. Each night either Jim or I went to visit him to see if his condition had changed in any way. His dear friend Ann Docherty was almost constantly by his bedside. Ann looked after him well, and she had been close to him for many years.

One particular evening, Jim and I walked into the ward as usual. Ann was standing at the head of the bed stroking Albert's forehead. I joined Ann at the right-hand side of the bed as Jim made his way around to the left of Albert.

The three of us stood there in silence, looking down at our dear old friend. I guess it must have been at the end of the visit when I began to sense the presence of a lady with long auburn hair standing at the foot of the bed. I knew that no one could see this lady, as she was obviously from the spirit world.

I looked across to Jim and then to Ann, for by now there seemed to be a feeling of intensity building around us. Albert began to stir. Still in silence, we all looked directly at him, not knowing what to expect.

By now the spirit lady had become so obvious that I thought the others might be aware of her presence. At that moment, Albert's eyes opened. He looked around at each one of us in turn, starting with Jim, who was holding his left hand. Then he turned his head to me, and eventually to Ann.

Lifting his head from the pillow, his eyes became fixed on the empty space at the foot of his bed. As if in a trance, his eyes widened and began to fill with tears. A huge smile broke over his face as he tried to pull himself up farther. Still smiling, with teardrops running down his cheeks, he said softly, "My wife is here." Both Ann and Jim turned their heads to the foot of his bed. "And my children— they've come for me." The three of us were fighting back tears. "You'll have to let me go," he whispered.

I couldn't hold back my tears another moment. The feeling of joy that was emanating from Albert was indescribable. Ann leaned down toward him and said, "We were never holding you back, Albert."

With this, he closed his eyes, and shortly afterwards went to join his wife and children, whom he hadn't held for 50 years or so since they'd died in World War II. God bless them all.

Albert left instructions with Ann that he wanted no funeral. He donated his body to medical research. Even in death his wish was that other people might benefit from his existence, something typical of this special man. Since there was no funeral service, Ann, Jim, and I set about arranging a service of thanksgiving for the life of Albert Best. So many people wanted to attend that we had to use the large church hall at the Glasgow Association of Spiritualists to accommodate the crowd.

Tributes were sent from all over the world. The people in the packed church listened as this humble man's great accomplishments were related, which dealt with stories of miraculous healings or wonderful messages filled with hope and love. All in all, I'd say that the service was a great success. The only mishap during the course of the night was discovered when the sound engineer, who was there to tape the proceedings, found that not one word or sound had been recorded on tape, even after he'd made several checks.

Albert Best had a marvelous sense of humor, and for this reason we kept the whole affair lighthearted. Many funny tales were shared by those who knew Albert as a clown, the role that he loved to play for others. He was never happier than when making others laugh at his expense.

Eric Hatton, then president of the U.K.'s Spiritualists' National Union, told of how Albert, returning home late from a trip, found that one of his friends had been in his flat and had left him some food for his expected late arrival. He was unaware that the kindly soul had decided to varnish the rather worn wooden toilet seat. The unsuspecting Albert found the need to use the shiny, new-looking toilet furnishing . . . and upon doing so, found that he was completely and utterly stuck.

After screaming out for an hour, Albert was rescued by his elderly female neighbor, whom he instructed to call an ambulance. The two ambulance drivers who escorted him to the hospital took great delight in making jokes about his predicament. But it was the doctor in the casualty department who added the crowning glory to this good deed gone wrong.

Albert, now lying facedown on a gurney, with the offending object fastened firmly to his bare rump, said, "I bet you haven't seen one of these before, doctor."

"Yes, in fact I see them every day," he replied. "But I must admit I've never seen one framed before!"

As this story was recited, I could almost hear the little Irishman's laughter from the spirit world.

✳ ✳

CHAPTER 7

FUNNY MOMENTS

Please don't get me wrong. I don't make fun of mediums or Spiritualism, especially when true and sincere practitioners are helping many individuals who really do need support at difficult times in their lives. But humorous situations sometimes arise when people are trying desperately to be serious.

One of Albert Best's greatest features was his ability to laugh, both at himself as well as some of the ridiculous situations he found himself in. Albert told me the following story.

He had just sat down after demonstrating his unique gift of clairvoyance to a packed London church when his very gracious hostess arose to thank him, and to inform the congregation that Albert would be available for private sittings the following day. Whatever the hostess had intended, what she actually said was, "Ladies and gentlemen, I'm sure you will all join with me in thanking Mr. Best for his excellent demonstration of mediumship. Furthermore, I take great delight in announcing that Albert will be holding his privates for three hours tomorrow morning. If anyone would like to book a session with him, please see me at the close of the service."

Albert told me he had a vision of himself cupping his "privates" and charging ten pounds for half-hour sessions!

What made this even funnier was that at no time did the hostess realize her mistake, much to the delight of all assembled.

Another slip of the tongue that caused hilarity among a group of Spiritualists occurred in our development circle in West Princes Street on a Thursday night. At the end of a circle, the leader would ask each person if they had a message for anyone else in the group. On this particular evening, one lady got to her feet and approached the gentleman who was sitting opposite her, who was wearing a very obvious hairpiece. When our would-be medium began to give her a message, it was apparent that she couldn't take her eyes off his thick, black head adornment.

"When I looked at you," she said, "I was aware of North American Indians dancing around you." Still looking at the wig, she added, "Then there was a great scene of the whole tribe."

"The whole tribe," the man repeated rather doubtfully.

"Yes," she replied, "they were dancing around a toupee."

Everybody in the room tried to muffle their laughter, hoping not to embarrass the poor man. As quick as a flash, he came back with a clever reply that gave him the last laugh, saying, "I think, my dear, that the word you are looking for is *tepee*. But thank you for your message. The Indian you saw must be the one who scalped me."

The entire room erupted with laughter, as you can imagine. Some of the funniest things in life seem to happen out of embarrassing situations, although to be honest, I don't know who was the most embarrassed in the end!

❊

The idea of having your own spirit guide has always aroused interest among Spiritualists. The very thought of someone watching over you is comforting. Guardian angels, guides, and highly evolved spirit teachers are sought after when people first begin their spiritual journey. The way some people describe their spirit guides can be quite hilarious, especially when you add in a generous slice of Glasgow patter.

I was sitting in the tearoom of a Spiritualist church in the East End of Glasgow one Sunday evening at the end of the service, when I overheard a conversation between a couple of elderly ladies. I will call the first lady Jeannie and the second Betty.

Jeannie: Hey, Betty, see your guide. He's a big stouter, so he is.

Betty: Aye, 'e's some size a man, in't 'e?

Jeannie: It's no rat. It's the size o' 'is weapon.

Betty: Aye, yur right. It's a cracker. I've held it, so ah huv. An' did ye see 'is feathurs?

Jeannie: Oh, they wur beautiful, so they wur. He wiz covered in thum. Heed tae fit.

Betty: Some o' these Indians ur magnificent specimens of manhood, so they ur.

Jeannie: Well, ah don't know how a wee wumin like yursel kin let a big man like rat cum throo' 'ur.

Betty: Ach, wance ye get usedntae it, it's no rat bad, ne'er it is. Beside all ma guide's ur big men.

Jeannie: Oh, yur dead lucky, you ur, mine ur aw wee wumen.

I wonder what the guides were discussing while this conversation was taking place. Perhaps they were comparing weapons and rosaries!

Tricia Robertson, of the Scottish Society for Psychical Research, told me a funny thing that happened when she and Professor Archie Roy were asked to investigate a haunting in a pub in Glasgow. Apparently, most of the bar staff had experienced strange and eerie feelings in certain parts of this public house. After much complaining to the manager, he finally agreed to call in the psychical researchers.

The only time that Tricia and Archie had available to investigate this so-called haunting was Friday around lunchtime. You can imagine how busy the pub was. Having been advised by the manager to be discreet about their investigations, Tricia told Archie to have a seat in the corner out of the way while she had a quiet word regarding ghostly disturbances with the man in charge.

As she pushed her way through the packed establishment, she managed to catch the attention of one of the staff, a young female whose mind was occupied with large orders for drinks. "What, hen?" she shouted to Tricia over the noise of the crowded bar room. Tricia, trying her best to be discreet, said, "I'm here about the disturbance."

"Aw, hen, you're in a pub. People are allowed to make noise," she answered, not really getting the message the first time.

"No," Tricia continued, trying her utmost not to give the game away to all the customers, "Professor Roy and I have been called in by the manager to help with the other disturbances." She winked at the bemused girl.

Suddenly the lightbulb went on as she finally realized the nature of Tricia's business. "Just a wee minute, pet, I'll get the boss," she said. Putting down the pints of beer she was holding, the barmaid cupped her hands around her mouth and let out the loudest shout possible, saying, "Sammy, it's the people about the ghost."

The whole place fell into instant silence, as you can imagine. Tricia said that the manager's head dropped into his hands in a gesture of disbelief at the young lady's lack of tact. Well, I would say that this was the time for a sharp exit, wouldn't you?

I'll never forget the night when a visiting gentleman asked the leader of the healing group if he might be allowed to work with our own church healers. After the visiting healer presented his credentials, along with a rather long lecture on his experience as a spiritual healer, he was invited to work alongside our regular healers. He chose to treat a man already waiting in the dimly lit room.

During the healing, the patient tried to protest that the healer was working in the wrong area of his body. "It's not that leg," the patient protested.

"Just keep quiet. I know what I'm doing. In fact, I'm a specialist in healing legs," the healer boasted. "The spirit doctor that works with me has performed many spirit operations on some of the best athletes in the country," he continued proudly.

It was not until the healing session was over and the lights had been switched on that everyone came to the realization that the leg the supreme healer "treated" for over half an hour was wooden! I couldn't help but say to my friend sitting beside me, "I don't care how long he works on the patient, that leg is definitely not coming back!"

Isn't it just ironic that those who profess to be great at their particular craft always seem to come unstuck, and usually in front of the very people they've tried to impress?

Spiritualism attracts some strange individuals from time to time, as I'm sure most religions do. One Thursday evening during a discussion group, the topic was how the knowledge of Spirit has brought joy into our lives. A very well-groomed lady, who was attending church for the first time, stood up and announced to the group: "I have a spirit gentleman in my house, and each night when I go to bed, he makes love to me." Now, what did she expect me to say to that? I had no idea.

"Is this something you would like us to investigate?" I inquired. She looked at me blankly. "I mean, I'm sure you're very distressed about this—"

She stopped me in mid-sentence. "Absolutely not, young man! I just wanted to let you all know how happy the spirit world has made me. After all, that's what you were discussing, is it not?"

I've said it before and will say it again: "There's nowt so queer as folk" (which basically means: People are strange!).

�֍

When I think of some of the things that mediums have to put up with—and in our own churches—what can I say? I think you must develop two things: the first is a very thick skin, and the other is a bizarre sense of humor.

People say and do the funniest things when they're in serious situations. Often spontaneous or off-the-cuff humor seems to appear more frequently than the spirit people do! As entertaining as it all seems, though, it must never distract from the serious business that's going on, although I'm certain that those on the Other Side get such a laugh at us, trying ever so hard to be spiritual.

It's my belief that your spiritual journey should always include fun. Let's face it—if the life to come is as gloomy as some religious people would have us believe, I would rather stay here. It's been the joy I've experienced in my development that has kept me on the spiritual path. This life can be so hard that there are times when this sense of joy eludes us. So whenever the chance comes to be happy, reach out and grasp it with both hands.

❋ ❋

CHAPTER 8

STRANGE BUT TRUE

Many people consider mediums to be rather strange. I don't see myself that way, although some of the episodes in my life since developing my mediumship have been bizarre, to say the least.

As I already explained, my life has changed dramatically since I put my gift to use. But if anyone had told me that I'd end up in some of the places I have or met some of the people I've encountered, I would have told them they were out of their minds.

I was brought up in a working-class area of Glasgow, with only average scholastic abilities. But now I was being invited to speak before an audience of academics at the University of Glasgow, and I was teaching seminars and conferences, instructing those who wished to learn about the world of mediumship and the afterlife. Sometimes I'd have to pinch myself to realize I wasn't dreaming. On the other hand, there were times I wish I *were* dreaming!

One of the most ridiculous requests ever made to me as a medium came out of the blue. I was working in the salon late one Friday afternoon—it was a typical day at City Barbers. The staff had lost most of their affability by this time, so shouts of "Next!" screamed from all corners of the busy salon.

"How dae ye wunt yur herr cut?"

"A short back and sides, please."

"Is 'at a number wan ur a number two?" referring to the level of the electric clippers. Discourse like this was being exchanged all around the shop. Everyone's intention was either to get home or to the pub. "Gordon, phone!" one of the staff members bellowed.

The voice on the other end of the phone was that of a foreign lady, requesting that I should leave my place of work immediately and join her at the Hilton Hotel, where she would be for the next four hours. There seemed to be no way to explain to this lady that I was at work and would have to get permission from my boss to leave early. Furthermore, there seemed to be no consideration for me.

"Tell your boss man to send you to me, and I will pay your wages," she said. After a few more words of banter between her, my boss, and myself, it was agreed that I'd be released early to try and pacify Madam X.

Try to imagine how I felt when I approached the front entrance of the Glasgow Hilton in my work clothes. I certainly got some looks from the high-class clientele, all dressed for dinner, as I walked through the grand lobby.

"Are you sure you're in the right place, sir?" the elderly concierge asked me in a patronizing tone.

"Yes," I replied. "I'm expected by Madam X in Room 1108, thank you very much."

It was at this point that I realized the anonymous lady must be of some importance, since the concierge almost fell backwards in disbelief.

The door of the room was open, and in front of me was a beautiful middle-aged woman, whom I instantly recognized. This time it was me who almost fell backwards.

"Please come in, Mr. Smith," she said, motioning me into the room. Her tone was more gracious now than it had been before.

"Thank you so much for seeing me at such short notice," she said gently. All I could do was stare, but I eventually pulled myself together, for I was here to give this lady a private sitting. Almost as soon as I tuned in, the spirit people came though and spoke to her. During this time I forgot that she was someone of importance.

After giving her evidence from her loved ones on the Other Side for almost an hour, I paused for a moment and asked my sitter if she had any questions about her sitting.

"Yes, I do," she said, frowning at me. "I need you to ask your spirit people if they can assist my husband."

"In what way, Madam?" I asked.

"Well, it looks as if there's going to be a great public scandal concerning him. What I want you to do is to ask the spirits to influence some people's minds so that it— "

"I'm very sorry," I stopped her in mid-sentence. "I cannot do such things."

"I know it might sound a little bit immoral, but I will pay you well."

"Madam," I said, "you don't seem to understand me. When I said I couldn't do it, it's not because of any immorality. The fact is, I don't have the *power* to do it."

"But you speak to them. Won't they help me if you ask them on my behalf? I mean, my husband could be ruined if you don't."

I really couldn't believe this. Here was this high-powered lady, whose husband held a very important position in the running of their country, pleading with little old me to call on the spirit world to sort out an impending scandal! The only thing I could offer her was prayer, although some kind of counseling might have been called for, too.

"I will ask that prayers be said for both you and your husband," I promised. "If it is God's will, then nothing will come of the other matter." It's not too difficult to see how Rasputin misguided the Romanovs!

Fortunately, I never heard anything about the particular scandal. I guess the prayers did the job—or, if not, there was a hefty pay-off! Needless to say, I still get calls from Madam X when her country is in need of prayers, shall we say. . . .

*

The more self-aware I become, the more I discover that there are many paranormal activities going on around us. I've always been fascinated by the predictions that have followed me through life. Words such as *coincidence* are no longer sufficient when the evidence is supported by fact. The following account is not so much strange but true—and it's nice as well!

Dronma, my Tibetan Buddhist friend, is a very gifted psychic artist. During our development circle, she sometimes tunes in, and on occasion draws a spirit person who wishes to be sketched. On the evening of December 8, 1995, Dronma was showing the group drawings of spirit people she's drawn. Then she said, "Oh, yes, this one," turning the page of the sketch pad. "I don't know why I drew this at all."

It was a detailed drawing of a springer spaniel. After we all agreed how cute the little pup on the pad was, Dronma said, "I don't think this is a spirit dog. This little thing is seen in the drawing, sitting at *your* door, Gordon." In fact, the door behind the dog was similar to mine. Before we moved on to the next drawing, Dronma told me to look at the little barrel hanging from the dog's collar. "Although it's a pencil drawing, I feel that the little barrel is red," she said. Dronma then dated the page as she does with all her drawings, and that was it.

Almost nine months later, I received a call from my good friend June Oakley, an excellent clairvoyant, who lives in Leicester in the Midlands. Occasionally June and I chat on the phone, keeping each other up-to-date on what's happening on either side of the border. Out of the blue, June said, "Gordon, you're going to be offered a puppy. It's a spaniel pup. I'm being told by my friends in the spirit world that you must accept this little dog."

"Well, June," I joked, "whoever is telling you this had better find another home for it, because there's no way I can have a dog at this time."

"Oh, well, dear, that's what they said," June finished.

A week later, after speaking at a seminar in Glasgow, a lady approached me, asking if I knew of anyone who would be willing to give a little dog a good home. It never occurred to me that this could be the dog in my message from June, and I'd long since forgotten Dronma's psychic drawing.

"It's just that the little dog will be put back in the dogs' home if no one takes him soon," she said woefully. I apologized for not being of any assistance and then suddenly remembered the telephone conversation.

"Wait," I called after the lady, who had started to walk away. "Is this dog a spaniel?"

"Yes, as a matter of fact it is," she said.

I made an appointment to see the dog, with the agreement that if he were friendly, I would consider taking him home with me.

Well, I'm a typical sensitive—as soon as I laid eyes on this energetic ball of fur, with his long ears and sad, cheeky face, I had to have him.

His name is Charlie, and most people refer to him as Cheeky Charlie. I must admit that he hasn't been the easiest of pets to break in. It's because he was so lively that his previous owners wanted to get rid of him. He'd had three different owners in his nine months of existence. After he'd eaten a hall carpet and chewed his way through a door and just about every shoe in the house, Cheeky Charlie finally began to settle down with me, thank God.

About a month after he arrived, his kennel papers were sent to me, along with all his veterinary records. As I was going over the papers, I noticed that Charlie was born on December 8, 1995—the very day that Dronma drew the little springer in our circle. Further confirmation was the little red barrel hanging from his collar!

So I suppose that Charlie isn't just a dog, but also a living prediction that I'm now so glad came true. Maybe I should have changed his name to Déjà Vu!

❊

Have you ever tried to help someone, only to find that the assistance you gave caused more trouble than it was worth? Well, that's what happened to me when I tried to locate a diamond bracelet for a very distressed lady.

I'd just arrived at work when the woman who owned the newsstand across the street asked if I could give her a moment of my time. Not really knowing what to expect, I agreed. When I walked through the door of the small establishment, I was greeted by the lady's husband, a rather intent-looking man in his early 40s. As I approached him, he dropped his eyelids in a gesture of disgust and motioned me into the back, where his wife was looking very upset.

"Oh, Gordon," she said, "I don't know how to ask this as I'm not really sure that I believe in what you do—"

"No, we don't believe in what you claim to do," her husband interrupted.

You had to see this man to believe him. He was so straight and serious that I even felt threatened by the sharp crease running down the front of his trousers. His hands were cleaner than a priest's. I felt as if I was standing in front of a headmaster.

"Please let me explain," she went on. "We cannot find a very expensive diamond bracelet—"

"No, *you* cannot find the bracelet, you stupid woman!" the husband interrupted.

"Look, what is it you expect me to do for you?" I chimed in.

"Well," the lady pleaded, "I've been told that you're psychic, although I don't know if we believe in that."

"Oh, just get to the point, would you?" the husband squawked. All of this was before the first cup of coffee and cigarette that I normally require to get me started each day!

The gist of the matter was that the lady had misplaced a very valuable bracelet that hadn't been insured. I was required to find this by means of psychic deduction.

"Let me ponder on this for a short while, and I'll get back to you if I can be of any assistance," I offered. What I really meant was, "Let me get the hell out of here and have a smoke and some coffee!"

When I returned to the salon, I chuckled to myself as I thought about the ridiculous situation I found myself in. Even though it was laughable, I felt I had a duty to try to tune in and see if the spirit world would help the lady. After all, the husband seemed to be a difficult man. If I could assist in some way, this poor woman might be saved at least some of his recriminations.

"Come on, spirit friends," I said. "Help a lady in need. After all, if this item of jewelry isn't found, she might end up as a message from *your* side!"

It was quite amazing. As soon as I closed my eyes, there was a man and woman standing in front of me. They told me that they bought the bracelet for their daughter's 21st birthday, and then proceeded to show me where it was in the house of the warring couple.

I walked swiftly across the street to the newsstand and relayed the following: "You live in a white bungalow. As I walk through the front door, I can see before me three doors to my left and two doors to my right. The first door on my right is a bedroom, which is occupied by your mother-in-law."

"That's quite correct," said the astonished-looking lady.

"As I enter this room, I'm aware of a cream-colored carpet and bedroom furniture that matches. There's a window to my extreme right, where there sits a chest of five drawers. In the top drawer, there's some underwear. This is where your bracelet is."

"That's amazing!" said the lady.

"I hope I'm correct, but that's what I get," I said. With this, I left the shop and returned to work. Within half an hour, I had a phone call from the lady. She was in tears, telling me I was right. The missing object was in said chest of drawers in the top drawer as stated.

At lunchtime, I walked into the woman's store to find the couple engaged in a shouting match.

"Well? Have you had him in our house or haven't you?!" the husband was demanding.

"No, of course I haven't, dear."

If the man hadn't been so aggressive I would have laughed.

"You!" he screamed. "How could you describe my home if you haven't been in it?"

There seemed to be no way to explain to the man that the parents of his poor wife were anxious that she find the item so she wouldn't face a scene like the one she was presently enduring. Instead, I just asked to buy some cigarettes and said, "Thanks would be nice!"

At the end of the day, the gentleman apologized and thanked me kindly, finishing with an offer of employment. A friend of his who worked for an oil company might offer me a position dowsing for oil. I wonder if you can guess what my answer was? As I've thought on a thousand occasions, there's "nowt so queer as folk."

※

I'm now 41, and I'd have to say that I've experienced a good share of strange happenings in my life. But by far the most unusual occurrence goes back to around 1991.

It was just after 6 P.M. one Sunday evening when the mailbox on my front door was rattled.

"Gordon, will you come over to see my dad?" Standing in front of me was a child whose face was filled with excitement, and she was panting breathlessly. "Hurry, hurry!" she said. Her tiny hand pulled at mine with such urgency that I wasted no more time asking questions, but followed the child across the street and up the stairs of a gray apartment building.

This was one of the children in a neighboring family whose mother had been killed in a horrific road accident the previous week.

When we arrived at the front door of the second-floor flat, the child pushed it open and called out to her father, "Da, he's here! Come on in, Gordon."

In the sparsely furnished flat, there were five people—the two children, their father, the man who lived in the flat below, and myself. I was in the middle of inquiring about the urgency of the situation when the children's father stopped me.

"It's started again," he said. As he uttered those words, loud rapping noises began to sound all around the living room.

"You see!" the man said to his downstairs neighbor.

Apparently, the neighbor had been complaining about the loud banging sounds that seemed to come from the flat above. These started around midday and continued until that moment at intervals of around 20 minutes.

I'd been asked to check out so-called haunted houses before, but in most of these cases, sounds like the ones we were currently hearing could be explained as faulty central-heating mechanisms or the movement that occurs in old buildings. What made this phenomenon different was that there was an intelligent system of rapping that seemed to respond to questions that were asked. There was also an intensity about this place that I'd never experienced before. You could feel the presence of someone in the very atmosphere. What happened next took each of us by surprise.

As we were standing around discussing the sounds coming from the walls and floor, the carpet and everything on top of it lifted—the furniture, the three adult men, and the two children. It just lifted, with all of us on it!

This occurred several times in the course of about three minutes. It felt as if we were standing on some kind of surfboard, being lifted on a wave. The only information I can divulge about the next ten minutes is that at all times there was a beautiful sense of peace accompanying each wave of phenomena, and that we were given a most out-standing communication from the recently deceased lady. This was of a very personal nature. Such communications are intended only for those to whom they can bring love (and in this case, hope), and who might understand the nature of the message—a message that contained some unfinished business.

I believe that the power of love can move many things on Earth, whether or not that love comes from someone living in this world or beyond the veil of death. Who am I to say? What I *do* know is that there really are many strange things between heaven and earth.

❋ ❋

CHAPTER 9

UNFINISHED BUSINESS

It has been my greatest joy to share my gift with those who most appreciate its worth. Among them are people from all walks of life, from the richest to the poorest, taking in many noted and renowned personalities. The one aspect they each have in common is that all of them have suffered a deep loss at one point in their lives.

The difference between evidence from the spirit world that's said to be general and that which is considered specific is a matter of unfinished business. I've experienced many cases of spirit contact where the deceased has passed to the Other Side in such an abrupt manner that they find themselves filled with a sense of urgency to contact their loved ones on the Earth plane. It's as if they have a need to console grieving relatives with the news of their survival.

Of the thousands of messages I've passed on from the spirit world, most seem to confirm that no matter how a person dies, their spirit arrives on the Other Side intact, without having experienced the pain and torment that we on the Earth plane imagine they felt.

When someone who has died suddenly manages to come through to a loved one, they normally bring back a message of great significance. Can you imagine the look on a mother's face when her murdered child returns to tell her how she's survived death and that she loves her—and then is able to back this up with information that only the grieving parent can understand? Or a woman whose husband went to work in the morning and didn't return in the evening? If he can communicate words of comfort and guidance to her, she'll be able to go on living instead of wasting away with grief. In cases like these, a medium's work is seen at its best.

Experiencing this type of sitting many times, I've come to realize the value of the work that the spirit world does for the bereaved, and feel honored to be used by it. During this kind of private session between medium and sitter, there's no audience—no one but the sitter's spirit friends are looking in. Being able to help people in this way is the motivation behind my mediumship. If I ever feel like giving up my work as a medium, the spirit world usually steps in.

One sitter the spirit world sent to me certainly reminded me about the reason for my work just at the point when I was about to give it all up . . . those above have impeccable timing.

It was at the end of August 1997 when I sat in my front room waiting for Mrs. Lee Bright. The caretaker of the Spiritualist church had set up this appointment while I was on vacation. For me, it was a case of waiting to see who would be the next sitter. Would this lady really need to have a sitting with a medium, or would she be someone who wanted to know if she should get married, divorced, or whatever?

When Mrs. Bright eventually arrived, I knew instantly that this sitter truly required help, although the look on her face told me that she didn't expect me to be so young. It was an expression of shock, one that said, "What am I doing here?" It was clear to me that she hadn't sat with a medium before, so I did my best to reassure her, and the sitting got under way. I will allow Mrs. Bright to describe to you in her own words what happened.

On June 20, 1997, my younger son, Alan, died in a car accident, just one month past his 29th birthday. Only someone who has suffered the same loss can come anywhere near understanding the devastating pain this caused us. As a mother, I felt I had let Alan down by not being able to prevent this from happening: I should have been able to protect him, as I did when he was a child.

This is irrational, I know, but reason plays very little part in one's thinking at a time like this. The weeks following Alan's death passed in a mist of pain and anger—anger that such a fine young man should have been taken away from us in what seemed like such a senseless way, and anger with God for not protecting him, as I had prayed each night that He would protect my sons.

Pain enveloped us every waking moment, yet was still able to pierce us to the heart when we realized it was not a bad dream—the unthinkable really had happened. My husband, Syd, and I had lost a much-loved son; Iain had lost the brother he loved; and Sarah had lost her husband of just three years.

Six weeks after Alan died, we were to go down to Hampshire for the interment of his ashes. At this point, I found life so difficult. I had a desperate need to know that Alan was safe, as silly as that may sound. I've always believed that physical death is not the end for us, but until now that had only been an emotional belief. Now I needed evidence of survival of the spirit.

I telephoned the Spiritualist church on Berkeley Street and asked if I could please arrange a private sitting with someone. It was my great good fortune that Jim, the caretaker, arranged for me to see Gordon Smith, and from that very first meeting I've felt blessed that he was the person I saw.

Gordon was immediately able to make a link with Alan in such a way that I had no doubt that Gordon could hear him. It was an unbelievably emotional sitting for me, but I came away from it with a serenity I would not have believed possible that morning when we set out. I still wept buckets, but could tell myself that Alan was safe—not only safe, but happy. This can be a difficult concept to accept, I know, as on the one hand, of course, I'm glad that he's happy, and yet I miss him so dreadfully.

During the sitting with Gordon, he told me that two ladies had been with Alan after the accident, and one had been holding his hand, which was exactly the case. He went on to describe the spare bedroom Alan used as a study, and told me that Alan said I had moved the papers around, as indeed I had in order to find insurance and registration documents for the police.

Gordon also explained that Alan had been with me when I went through his wallet looking for his credit card, as I'd been asked to do. This was important to me because both Iain and Alan knew they could leave wallets or even letters or diaries lying around and I wouldn't look at them. I have a great belief in one's right to privacy. I suppose a *skeptic would say one could guess that naturally families would go through papers, etc., at such a time and, of course, that is true. But no one could give by chance a detailed description of a room they've never seen.*

At later sittings with Gordon, I had even more conclusive evidence that Alan's spirit still lived. There's absolutely no point in looking for earth-shattering pronouncements from "the Other Side." What on earth would that prove? What I needed was personal proof that it was actually Alan who was channeling information to me through Gordon, and that is precisely what I received.

During one sitting, Gordon suddenly said that Alan had a very deep voice, as indeed he had. He said he had no idea why, but Alan was singing what sounded to him like a hymn, and then lah-lah-ed through the verse until he got to the last line, which was "To be a pilgrim." This made me laugh, because Alan loathed this particular hymn. He'd had a thing about pilgrims since he was a little boy.

I was somewhat surprised when Gordon told me that Alan was showing him the bathroom, the layout of which he accurately described, but then said we would come back to it. We carried on with the sitting, but eventually Gordon said he had to come back to the bathroom, but he was not quite sure how to interpret what Alan was telling him.

Very quickly Gordon had built up a good link with Alan and was able to tell me that Alan was laughing, so he wasn't quite sure what he was letting himself in for. The reason he was reluctant to come back to the bathroom was that Alan had told him there was a bird in there. Of course, people don't normally keep birds in the bathroom. I was stunned when I heard this because I knew exactly what Alan meant.

When we bought this house, we all had a laugh because the previous owners had put an image on the underside of the toilet seat's lid. The image was of a large winking owl—hardly a common bathroom decoration and certainly not something anyone could guess! This really hit the mark, because when we finally replaced the bathroom fixtures, Alan complained so much about the missing owl that I bought a small bronze owl to sit in there.

One thing Gordon said puzzled me. He said that Alan was showing him a doorbell, and I simply could not think what this signified. Gordon said not to worry about it and just keep it in mind.

I was longing to tell Iain all about my time with Gordon, but since he was going off on a trip, I knew I'd have to tell him by telephone. However, we'd promised to call in to see his wife, Sam; and his daughter, Bryony, on the way home, as Sam was also anxious to hear about it.

Imagine my surprise when we were leaving Iain and Sam's house to see a doorbell, where before there had been just two wires showing, since the door had been replaced some weeks previously. I asked Sam when Iain had fixed the bell. She told me he'd done it on Friday night, the night before I saw Gordon. Not only could Gordon not have known this, but I didn't know it had been done, which rather rules out telepathy, suggestion, or anything of that sort.

This incident of the doorbell may seem trivial, but it was so important to us, and in particular to Iain, who wanted very much to believe, and who was so close to his brother that Alan would know he needed proof.

Each time I had a sitting with Gordon, I left feeling that I'd spent time in Alan's company—it's just that I can't see him or hug him. The evidence Gordon has been able to give me has been outstanding. I've only been able to present a very few instances of it here. There have been no generalizations—It has all been relevant to us. In fact, it has not only helped me, of course, but I've been able to pass evidence on to my husband, to Iain, and to Sarah.

The effects are felt even outside the family. I was able to contact the young lady who held Alan's hand after the accident and tell her that he was aware of her being there. She was so glad to know this, as she had been undergoing therapy since the accident. Knowing she had helped Alan helped her. So the love Alan was sending to us allowed me to extend it to her, too.

Although there were many pieces of evidence I was able to pass on to Iain, I knew that he'd want to come with me to see Gordon at some point. It was exactly one year from the date of the accident that he did this.

We had a splendid sitting, with much of the evidence being directed toward Iain, who was both moved and gratified to hear Gordon repeat Alan's words. I felt right from the first time I had a sitting with Gordon that Alan trusted him and had a *rapport with him. The day Iain came with me was one such occasion.*

Having assured Iain on the way to Glasgow that there would be nothing "spooky" about the whole thing, we arrived at Berkeley Street. As we drove along looking for somewhere to park, he asked which house it was. I had to tell him it was the one with white sheets draped over the railings! The church was being decorated. Then we went downstairs to the sitting room, which I was amazed to find was almost in darkness. This was quite the opposite of how the room usually looked in the early afternoon.

When I spoke to Gordon later, he had no idea why he drew the curtains on this particular day. He simply felt that he must. I'm sure that Alan found it highly amusing to watch Iain's reaction to the scene he found. It did not put him off, however, and he soon felt as strongly as I did that Alan was with us. In fact, when we came out, he gave me a hug and said, "Mum, we've been talking to Alan."

The evidence Gordon gave Iain that day had a great effect on him. He was hurting so badly due to the loss of the brother he was so close to and with whom he'd shared so much. Through the generous sharing of his outstanding gifts as a medium, Gordon has made it possible for us as a family to go on. He's shown us beyond the shadow of a doubt that our spirit does live on, and that Alan will always be with us.

It's a rule of mine to never give more than two private sittings to any one person. In the case of Lee Bright, it was more to do with her son on the Other Side. Alan had assured me that his mother required an extra sitting and was sure his brother would be brought along, too. The look on his brother's face when he realized Alan was communicating really was a picture.

Alan is what I call a good communicator. He was so eager to come through when he got the chance that he was going to make the best of it. He's given his mother so much evidence that I can't even begin to remember. One thing that sticks in my mind happened on the second sitting I did for Mrs. Bright.

Mrs. Bright had just entered my house when I heard Alan's voice clearly call out to me: "Ask Mum about Macbeth." Instead of greeting Mrs. Bright with "Hello," I said, "What about Macbeth"? Her eyes widened with surprise.

"I've only just bought a copy of the book on the way here this morning," she said.

In the year or so that I've known Mrs. Bright, I've witnessed a great change in her. To see such an alteration in a person and know that in some way you've contributed to the positive change of direction in their life is truly wonderful. To Mrs. Bright and all others in similar situations, may God bless you and give you the knowledge that love never dies.

※

Here are two additional statements from people who have sought help from me. The first is from Malcolm Bryce, who contacted me after the death of his brother. The second comes from a fellow medium, whose work is highly respected throughout the field of Spiritualism. It just goes to show that even mediums find it difficult to tune in when it comes to themselves.

Here's the statement from Malcolm.

I first saw Gordon some five weeks after I lost my brother in rather sad circumstances. He'd had a very short illness and was only in early middle age. A great friend who knew Gordon was concerned for me because of my reaction to the death. The air wasn't clear; things were left unsaid. Two sides of a situation remained unresolved, and I was in distress.

My friend spoke to Gordon and asked him if he would give me a private sitting. Busy as he was, he agreed to do so. I'd never met him or seen him demonstrate before. A date was set for the following Tuesday, and that was the first I knew of the arrangement.

However, on that Sunday afternoon I was feeling very low and decided to go to the Spiritualist church at Somerset Place for the evening service. It was a last-minute thought. I arrived just in time and sat near the door.

It was announced that the medium booked to appear wasn't able to be there and Gordon Smith would speak and give the demonstration. He'd been called in at the last minute.

It was a warm and friendly meeting. I was intrigued to watch Gordon, who was to give me a sitting within a few days. Toward the end of the demonstration, he was giving information to an elderly lady near the front. Then, quite out of context of the message, he asked her if she liked music: He was surrounded by music, my brother's passion and his profession. She accepted the message.

Could she understand the number 18? This was my brother's birth date, which was only a week or so away. She would think about it. I was convinced the message was for me, but felt that I couldn't butt in. Gordon spoke so distinctively again about the music. I was excited inside.

"Wednesday is significant," he said, looking to the lady. Again, she gave a vague reply. On the previous Saturday evening a dear friend phoned to tell me her husband had passed away peacefully. That was also a reason for me being very low and sensitive on the Sunday. His funeral was to be on Wednesday.

I felt that Gordon wasn't convinced that these remarks were for this lady, but he carried on, then started a new message for someone else. I felt that my brother had been there even if I hadn't acknowledged it publicly. I left the service as soon as it was finished.

On the next Tuesday evening, I made my way to my friend's house and was introduced to Gordon. We chatted briefly, but I made no mention of my Sunday visit until after the sitting. We sat together and fell into silence.

Gordon then spoke of hearing music and being surrounded by lights—not spiritual lights but flashing, colorful disco-type lights. I felt that my brother was there, as all this was very significant. "He is with a lady with the initial 'A,'" said Gordon. Our mother's initial. "I'm being given the number 18." My brother's birth date, which had come through on Sunday.

"He's telling me 'Wednesday.'" I told Gordon about my going to the funeral the next day.

"No, that's not it," he said. After a few moments Gordon continued, "He's telling me Wednesday was the night you all spent with him before he passed." Indeed it was an all-night vigil. It confirmed to me that I wasn't wrong in my feelings on Sunday, and what good evidence this was—not only repeated, but explained.

Gordon continued to give me in total, 12 detailed pieces of information as proof of my brother's presence. These included a nickname, a significant reference to my sister, news that I was going on vacation soon, and a suggestion that it would be really good for me to get away for a change of scenery after the bereavement.

There was no specific mention of the unresolved matters, but the evidence and warmth of feeling coming through gave me great comfort. I felt there was an understanding that helped me reconcile the situation, to my extreme relief.

Since then I've seen Gordon demonstrate several times and had evidential messages from Spirit through him. On one occasion, Gordon was giving quite a specific message to a young woman. He then said that someone from Spirit was impatient and wanted to get through. It sounded like my brother, as everyone's timing had to suit him!

Gordon told the spirit contact to wait and continued his message. Within 20 seconds or so, Gordon apologized and said that this spirit person was so impatient that he had to interrupt. I told my companion, "That's my brother," and so it was. His personality came through before the message itself.

On two other occasions from the platform, Gordon asked if someone could accept a piece of information, a small but significant detail about a ring. I could, and each time the messages that followed were indeed for me.

What was remarkable was that the initial linking of such small details was exactly the same each time, and the two demonstrations were at least a year apart.

I value Gordon as a wonderful medium and now as a friend.

This is medium Mary Armour's account:

I first met Gordon one evening when I was serving the Jean Primrose church in Glasgow. I was invited by Mrs. Primrose to stay behind after the service and sit in her development circle. It became apparent to me on that night that Gordon had a gift far greater than any other in the circle. When I came home, I sent him a little card wishing him well and thanking him for the remarkable message he'd given me.

Over the years I've watched this young man of great ability grow from a fledgling into a spiritual dove. In my opinion, he's among the greatest in the world.

Now for some of the remarkable evidence and spiritual forecasts through the mediumship of Gordon Smith.

I've been fortunate to have three trance sittings with Gordon. He is, in my opinion, one of the few who at this time is a channel for the great materialization medium, Helen Duncan.

The first sitting when Helen came through concerned evidence about my father. It was known only to me. At the second sitting on January 27, 1997, Helen came through and said, "Mary, please be careful about your ankle." On February 14, I fell and fractured my ankle. In a more recent sitting in September 1998, he gave me a message from Helen containing information that I know to be true but, as Spirit says, the best evidence is that for which you have to search.

On the same night, Dominique, his guide, talked about a lady, Mrs. Jean Simes. I said I was sorry, but I didn't know her. But upon returning home, my mother asked about the sitting. I said I couldn't understand the last evidence received concerning Jean Simes.

"How do you know that?" my mother asked. "She died on Friday." Her friend Mary had told my mother about it the previous day. My mother was quite taken aback.

I wish Gordon well. As an ambassador for Spirit, the world could find no better.

❄   ❄

CHAPTER 10

LIFE AFTER DEATH

What's it like on the Other Side? Is there really life after physical death? Questions like these are put to me all the time. I guess that most people are looking for some form of solid evidence that will quell their fears of dying.

There *is* life after death. Of that I am certain. I've had so much evidence of survival that I can no longer say I just believe in the hereafter, for I know that life goes on after death. And there's an enormous difference between believing and knowing.

As for the question of what it's like on the Other Side, this is just a little bit more difficult to describe. There have been many different books written by people claiming to have journeyed to the spirit world, most of which describe a beautiful countryside with flowers and birds whose colors are beyond description.

It has been said there are great halls of learning, and hospitals where new arrivals can gain rest and recuperation. Stories are told of evolved assessors dressed in long white robes, whose role it is to help you understand the life you've just lived. There are descriptions of houses, cottages, and grand cities that surpass any in this world.

There are so many different reports and descriptions of the life to come, making it difficult to believe any of them.

It's my understanding that each individual interpretation is relevant only to the one who experiences it. Each mind will gravitate to a level of understanding most suited to its concept of Heaven, as it were.

It would seem that on the Other Side our minds progressively move away from material ideas. It's a bit like a snake shedding its skin as it goes through life. Once again, it reminds me of my spiritual development here and now, and how the most valuable lesson I learned was to unlearn and carry much less mental baggage.

I've had several experiences with the "hereafter." Each particular encounter with the Other Side has been incredible. Although in none of my experiences did I register anything of a physical nature, at all times I was in contact with the consciousness of different spirit people. The best way I can describe these encounters is to say that after each one I was left feeling more vital than ever before.

It's the most difficult thing to explain, for there are no words descriptive enough to adequately portray the images that you sense during these amazing journeys. The feelings of life and light are most predominant. On each occasion, I remember being aware of a strong pulsing, like a heartbeat. But this rhythmic sensation seemed to be in harmony with all of the different sensations of life that were present. There were times when I thought I was seeing someone I knew, but the sense of sight was so much more intense and went beyond the visual more than I'm used to.

It was the same with words, although at no point did I ever speak to anyone. Everything that was communicated between me and those I met was done by thought. More than that, on some occasions it was a communication of feelings.

One such spiritual encounter I shall never forget occurred on May 15, 1994. I'd just come home from a hard day's work at the barber's shop when I decided to have a nap before my evening meal. I lay on the settee and drifted into a light sleep. All sorts of trivial thoughts were passing through my mind when a vision of a man about 30 years old flashed before me.

I became aware of my entire body gently vibrating, almost as if the couch I lay on was swaying. At the same time, my mind began to focus more intensely on the young man, who seemed to be familiar to me, yet had something about his appearance I couldn't recognize.

There was a feeling so compelling about this man that I seemed to be drawn toward him in a strange sort of way. I'd known what it was like to experience an out-of-body state, but this was different. I felt as if I were traveling and yet was very aware of my body lying quite lifeless on the settee.

Then I felt a sharp pull around my solar plexus, and I was moving at high speed toward a light that appeared about the size of a pinhead. The entire episode felt like the sudden sensation you feel on the steepest drop of a roller coaster when it rushes toward the ground at high speed. All at once the rush was over. I had no sensation of my physical body.

The man who accompanied me through this state of altered reality was still with me. At first, he appeared to be in his early 30s, but when I was spiraled to his realm of spirit reality, I suddenly sensed him as a child of 10 or thereabouts. It was my cousin Stephen, who'd died almost 20 years earlier.

Stephen took me on a journey through this realm of spiritual beauty, which I cannot relay in words to anyone. All I know is that I was in a state of grace. From this point, I could understand life, love, and beauty in a way I'd never known before.

What I felt in this state was completely electric. As long as I live, I'll never forget it. The last sensation I can recall of Stephen was the sound of his voice just as I was about to wake from this between state. I remember it in the way that most people recollect their waking dreams as they emerge from sleep in the morning. Stephen was standing in front of me, smiling. Then he said, "I'll be with my mother on the 22nd of June." At this, I awoke with a start.

I couldn't fully take in what had happened, but the closing message stayed with me for the rest of the evening. I wondered if I should phone his mother, Sylvia, and tell her, but then thought better of it as it might disturb her. Instead, I wrote down the date Steve gave to me so that at some point in the near future I could ask his mum if it meant anything to her.

When I eventually got around to speaking with my aunt, I mentioned the particular date Stephen had spoken about. Sylvia assured me that it meant nothing to her. After this, I thought no more about it. I supposed it could have been a mistake, or maybe I misunderstood what was actually said.

It must have been near the end of 1994 when I next saw Aunt Sylvia during one of my visits to London. When I walked into her home, I was completely shocked to see this once very beautiful lady looking more like a victim of a prisoner-of-war camp.

Sylvia couldn't help but notice the look of horror on my face upon meeting her, and explained that she'd been fighting stomach cancer for almost five years. She was now at a stage where nothing more could be done for her. It appeared that she only had a short time left on the Earth plane.

For the next couple of months, I kept in constant contact with my aunt. I hoped to hear that maybe by some miracle or other doctors had made a mistake and that she wasn't as ill as they claimed, or perhaps an operation might be offered to give her a fighting chance.

But all the hoping and praying I did were to no avail. I was distraught that the woman I thought of as a second mother should have to face the same fate as her beloved son. Aunt Sylvia had changed her career after Stephen's death. She gave up a successful job in London and trained as a nurse. After qualifying, she then went on to work as a Macmillan nurse, serving patients suffering from cancer. (Macmillan Cancer Relief is a U.K.-wide charity devoted to supporting people living with the disease.) What a sad irony life can sometimes throw at us.

On Saturday, June 17, 1995, I decided to fly down to London, as I felt it would be my last chance to see Sylvia, who'd booked herself into a hospice for her remaining days. Before I left Glasgow, I bought two red roses. I put one into a vase at home; the other I took to London to give to Sylvia.

When I arrived at her room in a very pleasant building set in beautiful grounds, I saw my aunt sitting with soaking wet hair, waiting for me to cut and blow dry it! She said, "Gordon, I want to look my best when I meet Stephen," She was very strong about the whole thing. In fact, she refused to accept any form of pain relief, saying that when she passed on she wanted to be of a very clear mind.

Sylvia explained that she'd been with her son on several occasions, and that he told her he would be waiting for her to begin her new journey on the Other Side with him. Many people would say that a person in that stage of a cancerous illness would be hallucinating when claiming to talk to the so-called dead. I might be inclined to agree with them in some cases, but not in this one.

Sylvia was the most level-headed woman anyone could ever meet. Even in this state, she was able to arrange her funeral service as well as her own personal business. Not only that, but each member of the staff who looked after her in the hospice was called to her bedside one at a time, given an envelope, and thanked for their care and attention. No matter how ill she was, Sylvia was still very sober minded.

When I decided to leave later that day, Sylvia asked me to come closer to her. By this time she looked very tired.

"Darling," she said, "I'm about to take a step on a new journey. I'm not afraid. Please don't cry for me. Think of me being reunited with my dear son."

How could I cry for such a brave lady? As I was about to leave, I turned to her and said, "I'll see you around sometime." With this, she smiled broadly at me and retorted, "Well, if anyone does, I suppose you will, kid."

Upon returning to Glasgow later that evening, the first thing I noticed when I entered my house was the rose. It appeared to be dead, but even so I was reluctant to throw it out. I just stood and gazed at this once-beautiful flower, now wilting and deathlike. I could not help but compare it to the beautiful English rose I'd just left in the same condition a few hours earlier.

On the evening of Wednesday, June 21, I went to bed and prayed the same prayer that I'd been praying for the last week or so—that God would allow Sylvia gracious passage into the spirit world.

The following morning, I awoke suddenly to sit bolt upright in my bed. I immediately looked at my watch. The time was 5 A.M. I could hear a familiar voice near my left ear saying, "See you around, darling." It was Sylvia. She had gone . . . and on the very date her son had given me two years previously.

I waited until 8 A.M. to call my Uncle Michael in London, to be told what I already knew.

"Sylvia has gone," he said. He was broken-hearted to have lost someone as special as she was. Sylvia was loved by all who knew her, for she was a living angel. But this was an angel who was recalled to Heaven to be with the one she had lived without for so long. Michael continued, "She died at 5 o'clock this morning." I've often wondered how those in the spirit world know of such events so far in advance.

Later that morning, I noticed that the rose in my living room had come to life. It was in full bloom. It continued like this for another ten days before I reluctantly disposed of it. My uncle later remarked that the rose I gave to Sylvia seemed to die at the very same time she let go of this world.

This was a strange episode for me, yet just one of many I've experienced relating to life after death. I suppose that the most evidential experiences of the afterlife are indeed on a personal level. Albert Best, who also had so many encounters with the spirit world, would say, "Other than those who experienced it, who would believe it?" And, of course, he was right.

As I said earlier, people who find themselves in the spirit world seem to relate to all sorts of material things that can be found there. Given the evidence, it's my opinion that we create our own kingdom come, that each individual arrives at a place where they'll find comfort and beauty according to the state of their own mind when departing from this world.

With this in mind, I try to be careful of how I live my life on the Earth plane. This isn't for fear of retribution on the Other Side, but more for the ability to gravitate to a state of beauty there. There *is* life after death, of this I'm sure. But the important aspect to take from this knowledge is that the people who are left behind in this world must learn to go on with their lives after the death of a loved one.

There *is* a spirit world. And if you've created a bond of love with another in this world, then nothing—not even death—can separate you from them.

❋   ❋

CHAPTER 11

PROVE IT!

No matter how many times a medium provides sound evidence of life after death, there will always be those who insist that there are other more logical explanations than survival of the human spirit.

For more than a century, mediums have been investigated by men and women of science, whose aim it has been to prove or disprove the legitimacy of their work. As long ago as the 1850s, mediums such as Daniel Dunglas (D. D.) Home permitted some of the most eminent men of science to investigate their highly controversial mediumistic abilities.

It was due to mediums such as D. D. Home that the science laboratory and the seance room were introduced. Like all mediums who know that their gift is genuine and inspired only by a higher spiritual source, these early pioneers willingly allowed scientists the chance to attend some of the most famous seances in the history of Spiritualism.

I mention D. D. Home because in all the years he practiced his rare brand of mediumship, he was never at any time seriously accused of being, or found to be, fraudulent. Nor were his seances conducted in the dark. This Scots-born natural medium produced great feats of levitation and materialization in well-lit rooms in full view of many learned and professional people.

All in all, he was probably one of the greatest exponents of mediumship known to humanity. Furthermore, Home never charged for his gifts, yet another true mark of true spiritual mediumship. Among his countless sitters were the then-Czar of Russia and the German Kaiser.

Within the last 150 years, mediums such as D. D. Home, Leonore Piper, the Bangs sisters, Helen Duncan, Helen Hughes, Ena Twigg, Leslie Flint, Albert Best, and many more have worked so hard to prove that there's life after death. All of them brought comfort and inspiration to so many people, as well as perhaps helping science discover a little more about the nature of the human spirit. Each one of these mediums showed great trust in the gifts that they were given by God.

In 1994, I was asked by Tricia Robertson, of the Scottish Society for Psychical Research, if I would give a demonstration of mediumship at the University of Glasgow for Society members and the public. The event was to be hosted by Archie Roy, emeritus professor of astronomy at the University of Glasgow. I agreed without giving the matter much thought.

It's strange how I should perceive something as a challenge when it lies in the distant future, only to find as the time draws nearer that I wish I'd never opened my big mouth! It's at times like these that all of my positive energy starts to diminish and is replaced by negative thoughts and fears of how it could all go wrong.

What if nothing happens on that night? What if no one can understand any of the messages that might come through?

So many times I've put myself and my mediumship out on that same limb! I've gone through the same fears and concerns time and again, whether it be before working at the university or in a theater in Gibraltar, or even in some of the large halls I've demonstrated in up and down the United Kingdom.

The more I try to think about the outcome of such events, the more I end up a nervous wreck. At the end of the day, whether there *is* to be contact with the Other Side, and whether it *is* to be seen as good or otherwise, shouldn't really affect me beforehand. Neither I nor anyone else will ever change events in the future by worrying.

So here I was once again standing in a large hall filled to capacity, only this time most of the audience was there to investigate my work on a scientific level rather than out of need or spiritual fulfillment. All I remember about that night was Professor Roy's marvelous introduction of me. After that, I told the spirit people, "Come on, please don't let me down!" Of course, they didn't.

Following the demonstration, I was invited to answer questions from members of the audience. Most of them came from academic backgrounds. Strange as it seems, I was full of confidence after my successful display of mediumship. Besides, all I had to do was answer truthfully. Since that first night at the university, I've been asked back several times. On one of these occasions, the strangest thing happened. I certainly couldn't have planned anything better if I'd tried.

It was my third visit, and I'd been asked to take questions before the clairvoyance. A gentleman sitting in the front row asked me, "Gordon, is it not true that all mediums do is read body language accompanied with telepathic information that they pick up from the recipient's brain?"

"No, sir," I said. "For one thing, there have been many occasions where mediums—including myself—have given evidence to people that they knew nothing about.

"There are other incidents when the medium has provided information about someone else in that particular person's family that was taking place at that very moment, and the recipient was unaware of it. There are volumes of records held within the archives of the Society for Psychical Research in London with sworn statements to back up what I say."

However, we didn't have to wait long. The spirit world decided to prove my point that very night. I had only just begun the demonstration—in fact, it was the second communication of the night—when I became aware of a spirit lady standing beside me. She told me that her name was Anne and that her son was at the back. Mentally, I asked Anne, "How long ago did you pass?"

"Last week," came the reply.

Oh, dear, I thought. *There's someone up there who has just lost their mother.* I was sure they would still be grieving terribly.

"Is there a man at the back of the hall whose mother, Anne, has recently passed over?" I asked.

Silence.

Come on, Anne, I said in my mind. *Give me something else.*

"He's wearing my ring on the chain around his neck," she whispered.

"Is there a gentleman who would be wearing his mother's ring on a chain around his neck?" I asked.

Again, complete silence. *Right, Anne, I'll give you one more try,* I thought. Tell me where you lived.

"Maryhill Road," was her instant reply.

I passed on all of the information, adding the street name at the end. Still nothing.

"Okay," I said, "if no one can understand this, then I must move on to the next message."

Just as I started to walk to the other side of the podium, a voice in my ear said, "There he is." As I looked back to the farthest point of the large hall, there was a man's face looking through one of the glass partitions in the door. He was one of the university janitors, trying to have a peek at what was going on.

"That's Jim," the voice said. "That's my boy!"

"Please, could you come in?" I called to the unsuspecting man, waving him into the room at the same time with my hand. I'm sure he thought I was mad. Everyone in the hall turned to their left to see this rather embarrassed man of 40-something standing in his long, tan-colored attendant's coat.

"Is your name Jim?" I called out. This was a do-or-die situation for me. If this wasn't the son of my spirit lady, then I'd better give up.

"Yes," the man said in a quiet voice. He really must have been wondering what was going on.

"Please do excuse me, Jim. But are you wearing a chain around your neck?"

"Yes."

By now he appeared to be baffled by the proceedings. "Is there a ring on that chain that would have belonged to your mother?" As I finished, Jim was in the process of producing the two items of jewelry for all to see.

"Your mother's name—was it Anne?" I quickly continued. Suddenly, the look on the man's face changed from a look of bewilderment to that of a person who was very emotional. He nodded his head in agreement.

"Finally, Maryhill Road. Does that mean anything to you, sir?"

"My mother lived there," he said, looking completely astonished.

He was not the only one with a look of amazement. Once the information was accepted, Anne went on to give the most incredibly detailed message to her son, all of it personal to him alone. It seemed that he'd taken a wrong turn in one of the corridors and found himself outside that particular lecture hall wondering what was taking place that evening.

Once I delivered the message, I thanked Jim for taking the wrong turn and for making my message understood. I switched my attention to the gentleman who raised the point about body language and telepathy.

"Sir," I said, "I do hope this contact from the Other Side will answer your question. After all, I'm sure you'll agree that in order to read someone's body language, that person must be in front of you. As for telepathy, I think the person involved would have to be sending out telepathic messages in order that I, the would-be receiver in this case, might pick them up. Even so, it would seem unlikely that this man was even aware of any such practices taking place around him."

It's cases like this one that highlight spiritual mediumship in such a way that even the most skeptical of people would have to agree that there's something going on around us greater than we can conceive. Even some of the most learned men of science have had to accept that not everything has a perfectly logical explanation.

Nor indeed does the world of science hold the key that will eventually open up the doors to some of the greatest mysteries known to humankind. But maybe if people from all aspects of life who wish to unveil these mysteries work together in order to do so, there's a chance that the information will start to present itself.

Psychic research groups have been trying for decades to unlock some of these doors. As mentioned before, some of these organizations and societies have on file sworn affidavits by many eminent figures throughout the years concerning case upon case of psychic and spiritual phenomena that have happened before their very eyes. Some of these phenomena still await an explanation.

As a medium, I believe that it's my duty to assist these people as much as I can. If my contribution to science has even fractionally advanced our understanding of spiritual matters, at least I will have offered something. It's far better to have tried than to have died of ignorance, which to me is the way of those who won't even look at a subject for fear of change.

I've allowed my mediumship to be subject to experiments in the hopes that knowledge will grow from them. I've assisted the true seekers in tests, blind tests, and double-blind tests. It doesn't matter to me whether people believe that what I do is genuine or not. All I can say is that I try my best.

It's nice to know that there are serious-minded people who support mediumship. But those who don't understand it or who haven't even bothered to investigate what it's about really have no right to form opinions about the causes and effects of it.

Professor Archie Roy became convinced of the powers of true mediumship after having a private sitting with my dear friend Albert Best. He speaks openly of this in his book *A Sense of Something Strange*. Since then, he's become a great modern-day pioneer in trying to prove that there's life after death.

Both Professor Roy and Tricia Robertson are, among others, trying to establish a scientific approach to studying the evidence given by mediums to their recipients in order to dispel the age-old claim of the skeptic that information given by mediums is no more than general. The following is an account by Tricia Robertson from her book *The Truth Is in Here:*

PRISM is an acronym for Psychical Research Involving Selected Mediums. This is a research group that was set up to study paranormal phenomena, including mediumship, in a scientific manner.

One of the criticisms of mediums made by skeptics is the hypothesis that mediums' statements are so general that they could apply to anyone. Under the auspices of PRISM, this hypothesis is being experimentally tested using statistical mathematical methods.

The first phase of experimentation has used a large number of statistics, having been carried out over a period of two years or so. Using the first phase protocol, the results showed that mediums' statements to recipients were indeed meaningful. The odds against the results being due to chance are ten thousand million to one.

Gordon Smith was one of the mediums who willingly participated in this first phase. The statistical analysis of his results always showed a high degree of accuracy to the intended recipient.

It was because of the high standard of his work that he was asked to give a demonstration of his mediumship at Glasgow University at the request of the Scottish Society for Psychical Research. No one was disappointed.

❄

If I had a penny for every time someone asked me, "How does your mediumship work?" I'd be a very rich man! The fact is that my mediumship works differently each time I give someone a message. It would be rather too easy to say, "I'm clairvoyant, clairaudient, or even clairsentient," meaning that I "see," "hear," and "sense" the so-called dead. But there are times when these three aspects work simultaneously. I'm certain that all mediums are aware of this.

When I was a child and mediumistic phenomena took place in my life, I simply accepted it as being part of my nature. There was no question in my mind as to how these faculties worked—they just did. As with any gifts people possess, left to their own nature these gifts will nurture and function in the proper way. It would seem that if we try to dissect nature's gifts, we actually block their flow. Mediumship is no exception.

To hear spirit voices as a boy was as natural to me as hearing those of my parents and other members of the family. To see visions in my mind concerning the future or to sense deep emotions from other people was quite common in my childhood. Looking back, I can now see that when other people questioned what I was doing, it put doubts in my mind about what I was really experiencing.

Watching the progression of the many aspects of mediumship I've had in my life, I find that I have a much clearer understanding of how it works. Each private sitting or message at a public demonstration is completely different. Sometimes, I "hear" the spirit people. Usually, this happens when the spirit visitor was a very good communicator on this side. Hence, they'll still be adept on the Other Side, as we take all our skills—good and bad!—with us.

On other occasions, I might "sense" a spirit communicator yet "see" and "hear" nothing. Again, I feel that this is due to the personality of the spirit contacts. When just "sensing," all I can do is describe the feelings they emanate. After all, not everyone likes to say exactly what they're thinking, which is probably just as well sometimes! Those I "sense" may well best be remembered for their quiet personalities.

As for "seeing" spirit personalities, this faculty often accompanies clairaudience or clairsentience. As I said, sometimes all three work simultaneously.

What some people don't fully appreciate is that not only does the spirit person's personality affect the communication, but the conditions of both the medium and recipient add or take away from what could be seen as a good, clear contact.

If I'm not feeling 100 percent, messages from the Other Side may well be distorted, to a greater or lesser extent. This happens if I'm feeling exceptionally tired, stressed, or strained; it's a bit like a radio running on weak battery.

Sitters also play an important role. If they put up barriers, arrive in a very skeptical state, or are tight-lipped, with arms folded and face frowning in front of me, I'm more inclined to be put off. Those who seek help should at least arrive open-minded.

Each and every sitting ought to be regarded as something of an experiment during which the medium can hopefully merge the two worlds to prove survival of loved ones—and that they've retained their intelligence, memory, personality, and individuality.

No one can "call up" the so-called dead. Communicators return because of ties of love and affection. There's a reason for this. If mediums could dial up anyone at the drop of a hat, some far-off dictator would soon be trying to contact Hitler or Stalin, to name but two despots.

At the end of the day, my mediumship works best when there's a need for it to do so. I feel that the spirit world responds to those who are hurting. It's like a heightened feeling that switches on in response to emotional pain in the same way that animals react when sensing danger.

Be that as it may, I always seem to answer the question of *how* my mediumship works with another question: *Why* does it work?

❅ ❅

CHAPTER 12

MEDIUMSHIP

"What's that thing called that you do, Gordon, that religious thing, you know whit ah mean?" My mother still can't understand what I demonstrate at weekends. She normally tells people that I do something religious, but she isn't too sure what it involves. I find that quite funny, although to be fair to my mum, she's the first to say she's proud of me, even if she doesn't know why!

Some people think of me as a very spiritual person. If there's a spirituality that others recognize, it's mostly an inheritance from my parents. I've already mentioned how naturally kind they both are. But more than this, it's an accumulation of all their many attributes and wonderful traits and human eccentricities that have bred in me an ability to laugh through some of the most difficult times in my life.

I remember visiting my parents shortly after Dad underwent an operation to replace both his damaged kneecaps with plastic ones. After asking my dad how he was managing, I turned to Mum and said, "He's doing quite well, isn't he?"

She replied with her usual deadpan expression, "Well, if you really want to know what ah think, ah think that wee man is trying to escape from me bit by bit and he's gettin' rebuilt somewhere else!"

Then she looked at Dad and said, "Sammy, don't sit too near that fire. They plastic knees o' yours might melt." My dad just shook his head and sighed.

Between the two of them, you would have some great material for a comedy. But through every storm they've endured in their lives, they've held each other together and also helped many other people through hard times. I don't think I would have learned any more had I been brought up by Mother Teresa and Gandhi, although the house would probably have been a lot quieter!

※

Isn't it strange that just when you think you know where your life is going, just when you think you know who you are and what you want to achieve, you're turned in a completely different direction?

I always believed I would open up my own hairdressing salon and be highly successful, then settle down in a nice house in the suburbs and enjoy all the trappings of that success. But it's not quite that simple when you wake up one morning with spirit people standing at the foot of your bed reminding you, "Hey, you're a medium, so you better forget all of this and get on with it."

From living that very ordinary life to following the spiritual pathway, I think I must say that the latter is much more fulfilling. Having worked as a medium for more than one-third of my life, I've been very fortunate, if not to say, very well guided. I've been blessed with good, sensible teachers, and friends who have become like family. I've been taught how to become myself in such a short space of time. I've developed self-awareness, mindfulness, and self-confidence—all of which has changed my understanding of life entirely.

Becoming a medium has brought many beautiful changes to my life. Being able to share that gift with those who are in such emotional pain and allowed to witness the healing that takes place because of it is my greatest reward. And I find that I can never be despondent for very long. Almost every day I see someone who's suffering such profound bereavement, and this is a reminder that my life isn't so bad after all.

A medium's soul is much like that of the artist or musician. When you're in the flow of your craft, everything about you comes to life. There's a wonderful sense of magic about you and what you do. It feels as if you're creating beauty in the form of healing souls whose hearts have been broken in two.

The life of the medium is like the movement of waves: One moment you experience such highs, and the next you drop to the depths of emptiness because of the withdrawal from that high energy.

I once compared my work as a medium to that of a piano. Imagine a great master playing to an audience of hundreds. Every note the musician strikes touches the hearts of people in such a way as to inspire passion. But when the concert is over, the piano is once more an inanimate object, just an instrument devoid of sound. There's no great admiration for what you are, only for what you can do.

✳   ✳

CHAPTER 13

TRUE SPIRITUALITY

Whenever I'm asked to sum up the meaning of spirituality, I find it very difficult. What I understand to be spiritual may not be seen as such by another. The fact that you practice a religion doesn't necessarily make you spiritual, although I'm certain that spirituality can be found in all of the world's religions if you're sincere in your quest.

Since the day I first walked through the doors of a Spiritualist church, I've found that my mental capacity has expanded in such a way that I feel like a completely different human being. No matter how I try to explain this, even in the simplest terms, I still can't find a better description than the words that were written more than 50 years ago by the Reverend John Lamont, a close friend of Sir Arthur Conan Doyle.

As well as writing the world-renowned Sherlock Holmes stories, Sir Arthur was a convinced and dedicated Spiritualist, one who proclaimed Spiritualism's message from public platforms not only in the United Kingdom but abroad, too. Sir Arthur wrote several books on the subject, some of which are still in print, though, sadly, less well known than his fictional detective. Rev. Lamont told Sir Arthur: "Spiritualism has been to me, in common with many others, such a lifting of the mental horizons and letting in of the heavens that I can only compare it to sailing on board ship, living as a prisoner below deck with all hatches battened down, then suddenly one night being allowed on deck for the first time, to the stupendous mechanism of the heavens all aglow with the glory of God."

I would have to agree and say that this is how it felt for me. It doesn't matter upon which road you travel to seek your God, for all roads eventually lead to Heaven.

As I recall, there were no religious pictures of holy statues in our family home. Neither was there any pressure to attend church on a Sunday. Religion was not a major part of my early life. In fact, even in school, religious education amounted to a quick skim through the Bible, as most state schools in those days taught only the Christian doctrine. Eastern religions such as Buddhism, Hinduism, and so on, were completely denied to us.

As a medium, now I find that I'm intrigued by most of the world's religions and philosophies. In all of these great teachings, I can see that the most important feature is the need to promote spiritual awareness in the mind of humankind. It's my understanding that all of the true religions are connected by the same golden thread of spirituality, which one day may unite them all.

When I set out to discover more about spirituality, I began by reading as many spiritual works as I could. Reading books on such subjects could only satisfy a part of my expanding consciousness, so whenever I found a lecture or discussion group on any religious subject, I took myself along, hoping to absorb as much knowledge as my sponge-like mind would allow. So I decided to try a different approach. I did what most spiritual junkies do. I looked for a new fix—a meditation class.

In the Western world, meditation is sometimes taught by people who would not know spiritual enlightenment if it dropped on their head. On one occasion, I attended a so-called spiritual seminar run by someone who claimed to have become enlightened after having spent a couple of weeks in an ashram in India. I'm sure he recouped most of his airfare that day alone after charging us £25 (about $42 U.S.) each.

I listened to so much nonsense in the quest to further my spiritual knowledge that I began to realize that the only thing that was developing in me was a deep cynicism toward some of the aging spiritual hippies who claim to be avatars and gurus. In most cases, the "enlightened ones" encourage you to learn their own particular system of meditation.

One time I was actually taught how to repair my aura. (Apparently, it was torn.) This practice consisted of listening to taped music, visualizing a threaded needle, and sewing with rainbow thread two inches from my body. What nonsense! I never did return to the class after that, so from now on my aura will just have to go to the invisible menders!

There's a large market for spiritual products. It's easy to attain certificates in most complementary therapies, as well as courses in mediumship and all the various types of meditation. In today's spiritual supermarket, you can buy into anything from acupuncture to Zen.

I'm not knocking the practices or their true practitioners. It's more to do with the people who market them in Western countries. Glossy magazines, colorful pamphlets, and business cards are handed out at psychic fairs and seminars promoting the particular master of whichever craft. Even though there are many sincere people working in the spiritual supermarket, there are still those whose only objective is to make money from those in need.

With this in mind, I decided that I couldn't afford to buy spirituality. Nor did I wish to. After attending a few more of these ridiculous meditation classes, I was fortunate to meet a proper Tibetan Buddhist, Dronma, the psychic artist. It was this very humble lady who introduced me to the practices of her beautiful religion.

What I most admired about the Tibetan ways was how understated these very wise people were. The Samye Ling Tibetan temple in the Scottish borders is an exact replica of its namesake in Tibet. It's set in a beautiful valley not far from Lockerbie, a village better known because of the terrible plane crash that occurred there. With its Oriental-style golden roof, the ornately decorated temple is the heart center of this peaceful community. But it's the Tibetan Buddhists who work and practice their religion there who complement the rugged scenery with gentle harmony.

Whenever you want to know the truth about any religion, all you have to do is to watch those who practice it with sincerity. By spending some time with them, I was able to assess the simplicity of their ways. One example of how down-to-earth the Tibetans are was shown to me when a young lady turned up at Samye Ling claiming to be possessed by demons.

Upon arrival, she demanded to speak with one of the lamas, who, at the time, was digging in the garden with a few of the monks. The small shaven-headed man clad in wine-colored robes joined the distressed female almost at once. Upon hearing her story, he decided not to order any kind of exorcism or ritual. No, this wise man of the East instructed the lady to dig in the garden. Then she was sent off to clean the kitchen and so on for the rest of the day.

The following day, the lama visited the now physically exhausted woman to see if she was still possessed. Needless to say, she was too tired to think about such nonsense. As is the case with most of these so-called demonic possessions and other such fearful imaginings, the woman had been living in her imagination for far too long—and the best remedy for this was to get back to the real world and become well grounded.

The lack of complication among these people really inspired me to always try to stay down-to-earth. Spirituality, the Tibetan way is seen as simplicity itself. Their prayers and meditations are always dedicated to those in need. But more than that, the practical kindness common in this true temple of light was a reminder to me that even though my childhood lacked spiritual doctrine or dogma, the people who brought me up were as spiritual as the members of any religious group. This was due to their actions, not their training.

I believe that I've discovered the best place to begin looking for spirituality: in two words—*within myself.* Each one of us has the ability to discover the spiritual nature that shapes and molds our individual personalities. As much as religions and philosophies can steer us in the general direction of enlightenment, no one but the individual can truly understand their spiritual nature.

After much searching, I found myself confronted with the realization that my spirituality began with me. My whole life, I remembered, was a catalog of spiritual events reflected by people whose lives were filled with pain and suffering. My parents were compassion personified. Many of the neighbors who lived around us in Glasgow were just as likely to help another without expecting a reward.

Once again, I found that the answers I was seeking in my adult life lay somewhere in the past, and one of the most vivid memories I have of religion came from my childhood.

I remember sneaking into the Roman Catholic church at the end of our street. This grand building seemed huge to me. It was one of my favorite places to go. I can still recall the gruff voice of the old priest as he would expel me. "Right, Smith, get yourself out of here. You do not belong in God's house!" he would yell. His actions were quite just, because normally I would have been trying to steal the candles from the large box at the side altar!

On one occasion, I remember slipping into the chapel during a wedding service. It was always a great day on our street when a wedding was taking place. All the local children would gather outside the gates waiting for the cars to leave, as it was a tradition for the wedding party to throw money from the car windows as they drove off. On this day, I hid at the side of the large hall on whose walls there were many statues and colorful paintings.

The one statue that caught my attention was that of the Blessed Virgin. I can still recall the thoughts and feelings I experienced in that brief moment. The eyes of this lady seemed to be looking straight through me. The look caused a feeling of great sadness in me, yet there was also a peaceful feeling moving up from my feet. I could feel my eyes filling with tears, as I wanted to take away the look of pain that seemed to come from behind her eyes.

I think she reminded me of so many women I knew who had the same look of resignation and fatigue on their faces—my mother, my aunt, and so many females of that same generation whose lives were anything but easy. At that moment, I could have cried for the sadness of every woman in the world.

It was a strange experience for a young boy to have, and it had a great effect on me. For one thing, I stopped stealing from the chapel. Just the very thought of those eyes gazing deep into my soul was enough. I also believe that it was my first feeling of empathy. From then on, I began to look at people differently.

As I think about the many people around me in my early life, I am constantly reminded of the wisdom and true spirituality that were displayed on a daily basis. If someone in the community had a problem, they simply went with it to an older member.

Usually, it would be one of the older women who had come through just about every difficulty life could throw at her. She would be the equivalent of every type of counselor who's available today. It was her life experiences that formed her training, not some dry textbooks. The other great advantage of these times was that whatever money there was, there was never a reluctance to share with those in need.

All of the lessons in spirituality that I needed have been within and around me since the day I was born. There was often more spirituality displayed in the tenement streets of Glasgow than in most of its churches. Whenever I need reminding of this, I think of one of those very wise and kind-hearted souls who fought through life and still managed to give so much.

Her name was Effie Ritchie, a spiritual healer in our church. She didn't have a lot, but what Effie did have was yours for the taking. Effie gave the distinct impression that she was very tough, although the toughest thing about her was the life she'd endured. She'd lost many members of her family, including her beloved husband, Charlie, by the time I first met her. Not too long after this, she was told that she had cancer of the stomach.

I'm never so amazed as when I meet someone with a terminal illness who seems to give strength to those around them rather than receiving it. Effie was one of those people. In the face of everything she'd been through, she was able to make others laugh. One of the most amusing memories I have of this fantastic character occurred while she was in the hospital.

I went to visit my dear friend knowing that she'd just undergone major surgery to remove the cancer from her abdomen. When I arrived, Effie was still asleep as a result of the anesthetic. As I stood and watched from the foot of her bed, she seemed to stir. "Hello there, son," she whispered in a pathetic tone.

"Hello, Effie," I answered, trying to smile at her. She really did look like she'd come through the wars.

At the same time, a young doctor arrived at Effie's bed and had a look at the chart hanging on the top of the frame above her head. The poor woman turned her head toward the young doctor and let out a sigh.

Oh, dear, I thought, *she must be suffering.* Just then, Effie's right hand, which was attached by the arm to a drip at the side of the bed, lifted up toward the unsuspecting young man's groin area.

"Mrs. Ritchie!" he shouted, directing a startled look straight at her face. In a feeble little voice, Effie replied, "Oh, doctor, give a dyin' wuman a brek!"

I immediately burst out laughing, but the doctor took a bit longer to get the joke, it seemed. This was typical of the woman. I'm sure she only behaved in this way to make me feel better, as Effie was never one to look for sympathy, no matter what situation she was in.

Effie lived for almost five years after this operation. I'm certain it was her unbelievable attitude that helped her survive for so long, or it could well have been the way she described it the week before she passed away.

"Son, I was ready to go five years ago," she explained. "Since then, I've constantly asked God why He has kept me in this world. It's only just dawned on me that I had to suffer so long to end up looking the way I do now so that my family can let me go."

It's strange how some people have to suffer in this world. But I believe that because of this, others can learn and maybe suffer less as a result.

Effie Ritchie was one of the most spiritual beings I've ever encountered in my life. This wasn't because she could give profound answers to questions relating to the meaning of life. Nor was she the world's most saintly woman. It had more to do with her compassion for others, her natural consideration, and how brave she could be when faced with adversity. She became spiritual not because she tried to be, but because it was her way.

Whenever Mrs. Primrose asked Effie to close our church service in prayer, some people were so affected by the honesty of her words that they'd be moved to tears. She spoke to God in a broad Glaswegian dialect, as if she knew Him on a personal level. "God, gonnee help aw ra peepil that ur suffurin, an aw the poor wee kids that don't huv much in their wee lives. God be wae au them that's no got a bed this night, thanks God. Ah no yil dae the best ye kin. Thanks."

And she meant every word of it. Everything Effie asked for she'd experienced herself. It is my prayer that God will pray as hard for Effie as she prayed for others. May He bless her.

✳

You can't be any more spiritual than you already are. All of us are given many chances in our lives to feel what it's like to be spiritual. There are times that we act on these impulses, and there are other occasions when we choose to ignore them. Whichever we decide to do will no doubt cause an effect not only in our own life, but also in the lives of those around us.

Spirituality can neither be bought nor sold. It can only grow in this world or remain hidden. The choice is ours—either to live in a world more harmonious because of us, or one that's filled with ignorance that we leave unchallenged. Every day, life puts lessons in front of each one of us. The choice to learn our lessons or ignore them once again lies with us, no matter how we choose to live our lives. If you can, "Remember kindness."

❋   ❋

CHAPTER 14

WORKING ABROAD

I thought that when I'd worked the length and breadth of the U.K. I'd done it all. Not so, it would seem. The next challenge for my mediumship was to be found overseas. Abroad? Me? How would I pass on messages in a foreign language?

This new opportunity to expand my mediumship was due to my old friend Albert Best. He thought so highly of my clairvoyant abilities that he recommended me to churches and societies throughout the U.K., as well as some abroad. In a short time, I had offers to work in such places as Australia, the United States, Germany, Switzerland, Spain, and Gibraltar.

There was no way I could accept all of these offers due to work commitments at home. The only thing to do was choose those that would fit in with my already overloaded schedule. It so happened that the only dates corresponding with my schedule were those in Spain and Gibraltar. Once I accepted this offer, I wondered just what I'd done. This would be the greatest test of my psychic abilities so far—and I also wondered if I could come through this test a more accomplished medium.

Ray and June Smith run the Gibraltar Society for Psychic Research, and this very kind couple greeted me when

I arrived at Málaga Airport. For the next week, I lived with them in their beautiful villa in the picturesque hills of Santa Margarita in southern Spain, overlooking Gibraltar.

My first trip to Gib was very successful. Everyone seemed pleased with my style of mediumship. The Spanish and Gibraltarian people who received spirit communications all reported favorably on the evidence they were given. During that week, I gave 35 private sittings as well as 2 public demonstrations of clairvoyance. If there was a problem, it was only that most of the electrical equipment I came into contact with broke down. This was noted by Ray when he reported on the week's events.

"Not only did the microphone fail to work each time you held it, but our video equipment failed to capture any pictures at all," he said. "Furthermore, our audio tapes quit; they just ceased the moment you began to work." This is why I have no reports of what occurred on my first visit.

My second trip to the Rock was even more successful than the previous one. This time my demonstration in the John Macintosh Hall was only captured on audio. Even after many checks, the video equipment still failed to work on that night.

The following is the report that the *Psychic News* later ran on its front page. The punny headline was: **"Glasgow Medium Gordon Smith Rocks Them in Gibraltar."** Then came:

Ray and June Smith from the Gibraltar Psychic Research Society report that Scottish medium Gordon Smith made an immense impact on the Rock of Gibraltar this month.

Without Gordon's prior knowledge, the Portuguese Consul in Vigo had asked to attend Gordon's demonstration in the theater, and booked private sittings for Wednesday, January 14, as well as an interview with both Gordon Smith and Ray that would include Carlos Fernandez, who is a well-known researcher and journalist in the field of psychic matters.

By coincidence, on the night of the demonstration Gordon went directly to the Consul with a message, without knowing her identity.

"I can hear the name Cardoso," said Gordon. The medium then gave the name Anabela. The lady said that Anabela Cardoso was indeed her name.

Gordon continued, telling the lady that a man called Juan was communicating from the Other Side. "That is the name of my father," replied the lady.

"He is telling me that you used to live in America," said Gordon. "He tells me that he is very proud of the work you do, and that you are here tonight to write a report on the events of the evening."

"That is true," the lady replied. The lady's father then continued by describing how he had seen her putting aeroplane tickets on a desk top, then going into a bar for a beer. The lady laughed and said that indeed she and her friend had travelled by plane to Malaga.

With another contact, the medium asked whether anyone knew the name Miguel, who had been killed in Red Sands Street. A lady responded, saying that Miguel was her brother, and that the name of the road was Red Sands Road, not Street. As the medium gave the numbers 1–1, the lady understood.

"He's telling me that he will be close to you on March 15," continued Gordon. "That's my birthday," replied the lady. The medium surprised the recipient by telling her that she would enjoy herself in Australia. The lady told Gordon she had planned to go in the springtime.

"He has brought with him a young boy," Gordon said. "About one year old."

"That's my son," replied the lady.

Both the receivers of these wonderful messages were naturally in tears, overcome with emotion, as they listened to the medium.

Gordon went to another woman saying, "I have your niece here, who tells me she was killed in an accident five years ago."

The lady confirmed this, saying that she was her aunt. The medium continued, telling the lady she was wearing the rings that belonged to her niece.

Gordon described how the communicator was telling him that the niece was looking after Maria. The recipient replied, telling the medium that Maria was the mother of her niece.

Finally in this communication, Gordon gave the name Eva, and said that Eva was seventeen years old, and that her mother was starting to feel better about her.

Ray Smith states: "I know Eva's mother because in the past she has come to many meetings both in the centre and in the theatre. The mother's name is Marie Carmen, and she has been grieving ever since she lost her daughter in a motor accident.

"The Portuguese Consul did attend on the following day, bringing with her a friend who only spoke Spanish. The Consul acted as interpreter, and I understand that her friend had a wonderful sitting. I was witness to the fact that they both came out of the sitting room in tears.

"The contacts quoted are only a sample of those the medium gave. All the links made in both demonstrations, as well as in his private sittings, were of the same very high standard.

"I can assure you we have recordings and many witnesses to verify that all that has been reported here took place. I must confess I have not witnessed such good mediumship since the days when Gordon Higginson (another top UK clairvoyant) and Albert Best came to demonstrate in Gibraltar.

"In a sense, it seemed that Albert Best was helping Gordon with his mediumship. This is not surprising since they both lived in Glasgow, and Gordon has worked with Albert.

"In the opinion of the Gibraltar Psychic Research Society, Gordon Smith's mediumship was very good on his last visit here, but on this occasion he has surpassed himself. The request for his return was shared by all in the theatre when at the end of the meeting he received a wonderful ovation."

What was not in that report was the fact that I had to go on local television and do battle with a priest, who announced on the radio news that the devil had arrived in Gibraltar in the form of Gordon Smith from Scotland!

If that wasn't enough attention, June Smith asked me if, for effect, I would wear a kilt on the night of the theater demonstration. Wearing a kilt is one thing, but then I learned that we were to travel over from the Spanish side on a motorcycle, with me riding on the back of it. Were these Gibraltarians ready for this?

I'd never worn a kilt while riding on a motorcycle before, so I had no idea that the garment would be lifted up over my head, making me resemble a rather large red tulip speeding along at 50 miles an hour. The Spanish guards at the checkpoint were wide-eyed to say the least when the "devil" arrived wearing a red dress! Still, once we eventually got to the theater, the people really did appreciate the Highland dress, although, being a true Scot, it disturbed me that I could have been arrested for high-speed flashing!

Working with the Spanish and later the German people helped me gain even more trust in spirit communicators. It showed me that even the language differences didn't pose a problem for those on the Other Side, for messages of love and comfort were passed to relatives as clearly and accurately as they are in the United Kingdom.

All of my life I've noticed that even the most unlikely predictions have come to pass. So when asked to visit Japan to represent the London-based Spiritualist Association of Great Britain (SAGB), I simply remembered the prediction given to me by that wise old medium Albert Best, who three years earlier had said, "You will visit Japan within the next five years."

I should explain that the SAGB is housed in a beautiful Georgian building in plush Belgrave Square in the heart of London's Belgravia.

I often appear at the Association when it's holding a special public event, and I love demonstrating in the Oliver Lodge Hall with its grand piano, glittering chandeliers, original Adam fireplaces, and large windows overlooking Belgrave Square. Of course, as well as seeing friends old and new, it's also a marvelous opportunity to meet up with fellow mediums from throughout the United Kingdom. Another of the delights of serving the Association is the feeling of warmth and camaraderie between all who serve there. I really do regard it as a great privilege to call myself an SAGB medium.

But back to Japan. I only wish Albert had mentioned the heavy workload involved, then maybe I would have thought twice about it! On April 25, 1999, I flew to Japan with Hiroshi Kinjo, a spiritual healer at the Association. As well as being my interpreter, Hiroshi would lead some of the workshops, which involved spiritual awareness and healing.

Before we began our nine days of spiritual work, Hiroshi took me on sightseeing trips to many of the most beautiful and scenic parts of Japan. We also had time to visit some of the old Buddhist, Shinto, and Zen temples dotted throughout the countryside.

For me, these visits were the highlight of my sightseeing excursions. One temple was more beautiful than the next, all of them built in the traditional Japanese style, with gold sloping roofs and exquisite carvings and paintings. Equally as fantastic were the sculpted gardens that surrounded them.

I spent much of my time trying to picture the ancient peoples in their colorful costumes and robes roaming about these picturesque places, mindfully going about their duties. The gardens, and these peaceful temples with their backdrop of ghostly high mountains shrouded in mist and low clouds, were a complete contrast to the bustling streets of Tokyo. Here, there are buildings seemingly as tall as the mountains, streets aglow with neon signs of all colors flashing advertisements through the streets broad and narrow. All were crammed with millions of people going about their business like droves of ants.

From the top of the fairly high building where we stayed, I looked down on some of the main streets of this vast city and was amazed at the view below me. If Tokyo was the heart of Japan, these great floods of people flowing through its streets were the blood pumping around its veins. In all my life I've never witnessed so many people in one place at one time. The people of Tokyo seemed to be as concentrated on their business life as the monks in the temples were on their spiritual practices.

During the course of our spiritual work, many people came along to take part in workshops, spiritual healings, and demonstrations of clairvoyance. To our delight, everyone appeared to enjoy themselves at each event. For me, the amazing aspect was being able to hear and correctly pronounce the Japanese names of spirit contacts.

Since I don't speak Japanese, and 99 percent of the recipients spoke no English, this proved to be a great help. As always, the spirit people proved that they could bridge the language gap. Of all the many messages given in public and private sittings, there's only one that sits in the front of my mind. It happened on the second-to-last day of our work schedule.

Everything had gone well, with no hiccups. It couldn't have gone any better. In fact, Hiroshi and I had just commented on that. Why is it that whenever you have that thought, someone or something turns up to change it?

It was the last sitting of the day. Our sitter was a gentleman in his mid-50s who was very well groomed and smartly dressed. I had just begun to tune in when the man started to speak in a rather hurried fashion to Hiroshi. My interpreter turned to me and said, "He believes he's been possessed by an alien."

Apparently, the alien was lodged between his testicles and liver. He told us he had swelling around both parts of his body, and that his stomach would swell from time to time. I looked at Hiroshi in amazement, and he returned my look and asked me what we should advise the man. At this point, the man began to speak again. He went on for some ten minutes or so, explaining to Hiroshi how the alien had been transferred to him from a Japanese mystic. He seemed to be very well versed in mystical terms, as if he'd read many books on the subject.

I told Hiroshi to advise the man to see a doctor rather than a medium. Hiroshi passed this message to the man . . . who in turn told Hiroshi that *he* was a doctor! Upon hearing this, I almost laughed out loud. I believed that this man was suffering from "spiritual indigestion," the result of reading too many books on mysticism and enlightenment.

It was my opinion that the doctor should try to ground himself by living as ordinary a life as possible. I ended the session, and offered this poor soul spiritual healing in the hopes that he would feel more relaxed and maybe see his condition in a different light. Evidently it worked. As soon as the healing was finished, he announced that the alien had been reduced to one-sixteenth of an inch.

It's difficult to imagine that someone so intelligent could delude himself in such a way, although I found many of those we saw to be very superstitious. Several of them came to me hoping that I might be able to lift curses put on them or their family members. In all of these cases, all I could offer was common sense.

All things considered, my trip to Japan was a fascinating experience, even though I was very tired at the end of it. No matter where I go in this world or how enticing a place can be, it's always good to get back home.

But as for resting, there was no chance! I practically stepped off the plane and onto the platform. Luckily for me, I was sharing it with the brilliant young medium from Essex, Tony Stockwell. Tony and I seem to work very well together. At the end of our demonstration, he turned to me and said, "Did you know that you will go back to Japan?" A look of exhaustion came over my face. Tony smiled and said, "I'm just kidding." Thankfully, he was.

❊ ❊

CHAPTER 15

OF SEANCES AND SONS

"I was the best of kids, I was the worst of kids." I think that someone else wrote something like this once before, but was referring to "times." In my mother's eyes, I could do no wrong. Nor could any of her other children for that matter.

If any of us were to smash all the windows in every house in our street, Mum would have said, "It couldn't have been any of mine. It must have been kids that looked like them." If she was guilty of anything, it could only be of loving and protecting her family. And, of course, she did, like a lioness protecting her cubs. God help the person who tried to interfere with her children.

By the time I reached my early teens, there was a noted difference around our once very busy home. Both my sisters, Betty and Joan, as well as my eldest brother, Tommy, had by now married and moved into their own houses. This left Sammy, John, my parents, and me at home.

Sammy was just about to be given a room of his own when it was announced that Barney, my mother's father, was coming to stay. My grandfather was quite ill when he came to live with us. Indeed, he was now confined to his bed and could no longer live on his own.

Granddad was put up in our middle room, the smallest of the three bedrooms in our house, which meant that Sammy would still have to share with John and me.

The three of us used to drive my mum mental. We would play together for so long, then one of us would disagree about something or other and the fights would start. "Would you lot keep it down in there!" Lizzie would bawl.

"It's him, Mammy," one or other of us would yell back.

"Ah don't care whit wan it is," she'd reply. "I'll come in there and belt every wan o'ye."

Usually at this point we would shut up as asked, for Mum is one of those women who carried out her threats to the letter. It's no wonder, I suppose, when you consider that she was always busy cooking, cleaning, and washing, mostly for other people. The last thing she needed was countless distractions from three rowdy teenagers. "Why don't you all go outside and give me peace fur a while?" she'd ask.

One Saturday night after obeying Mum's orders to go outside and play, my two brothers and I decided to get some other friends and try to hold a seance in the old wooden hut that Sammy had built in our back garden. (This experimental seance was, of course, my idea, with me as the medium. Who else?) Two more of our friends joined us, making a gathering of five eager young minds hoping to pull back the veil into the Great Unknown.

The setting, I decided, was perfect. After all, the conditions had to be to my liking as I was starring and directing in this, my debut as the great mystical medium forecast by Sadie and Ella. Even the weather was perfect, as the night was dark, with a slight chill in the air.

Five of us sat cross-legged on the cold dirt floor of the shoddily constructed hut. In the center, there was a candle welded to an upturned soup can. The candle constantly flickered from the many drafts whistling in through gaps in the uneven planks of wood that made up our walls.

"Shush," I moaned. "If you want me to do this, you'll all have to concentrate." Silence filled the hut as I closed my eyes and addressed the space above my head. "Is there anybody there?" I asked in a serious voice. I swear you could have heard a pin drop. "If you're there, give us a sign."

This carried on for a few more moments, separated only by silence as the intensity grew. Here I was commanding everyone's attention, only there seemed to be no backup from the spirit world. It was time to improvise.

"I can hear a voice," I said, pretending, of course. "It's Sarah [my late grandmother]." Then the strangest thing did happen. As I continued with my charade, I began to speak spontaneously.

"I'm coming to collect Barney," I said in an unfamiliar voice.

"Whit diz that mean?" Sammy asked.

"I don't know," I replied.

"You better cut this out," Sammy said, sounding really annoyed as he raised himself to a squat position, which was all that the hut would allow. Then he pushed past me and left.

John looked at the two others and said, "It's all a load of crap anyway. He just made it up."

"The spirits don't lie!" I protested.

"Naw, but you dae!" John exclaimed.

The three remaining sitters burst out laughing and left one by one. Here I was, the 11-year-old medium, left sitting in my empty seance room. My thoughts were now filled with anxiety as I wondered if my brothers would tell Mum what I'd done. How could I have been so stupid to have said what I did?

The following morning, our bedroom was filled with light blazing in through the large double windows. John and I awoke almost at the same time. We decided to play with our table football game, agreeing to keep the noise down, as the rest of the family was still asleep. Typical of us, within five minutes or so we'd woken everyone up. "Would you two keep the noise down in there!" my mother shouted from the far end of the house. I immediately tried to mimic her voice.

"Shut up, you! She'll hear you." John scolded me for impersonating Mum.

The two of us were trying to muffle our laughter and still keep the game going when suddenly there was a scream. John and I were rooted to the spot. It felt as if a siren had gone off and we were waiting for the next sound to release us from our fear. Within seconds, everyone was in the hall.

Sammy had jumped out of bed, and John and I were rushing out of the living room where we'd been playing. My father was just coming out of Granddad's bedroom while Mum was standing at the door of her bedroom, at the end of the long hall.

Dad had gotten up to make a cup of tea for Mum and Granddad. Mum could hear him trying to rouse her father, when something inside her told her that he'd died. "He's dead, isn't he?" she asked. Tears were streaming down her face. I'd never seen my mother sad before. Somehow, I felt responsible. If I hadn't held that stupid seance the previous evening, none of this would have occurred.

The look of shock on the faces of my two brothers filled me with a kind of remorse. *Oh, dear,* I thought. *What will I say if they repeat what happened last night?*

I didn't have to be psychic to understand the seriousness of what was happening now. Dad sent the three of us to my sister's place. Betty lived around the corner from us, no more than a minute's walk from our house.

Betty's husband, Jim, stayed with us, and my sister went back home to be with my mother while Dad sorted things out. As the three of us sat there, I could tell by the looks I was getting that my two brothers weren't about to say anything about my prediction, although I believe it was more out of fear. I'm sure they regarded me as evil at that moment.

A week after Granddad's funeral, Dad began redecorating the middle room so that Sammy could move into it as soon as possible. John and I argued that we wanted a room of our own—just because Sammy was the oldest why should he have it? Sammy sneered at us from behind my dad's back. Meanwhile, Dad pointed out to us that it was only right that the oldest should have it. How quickly life goes on. Granddad wasn't even cold, and there we were debating to see which one should get his bedroom.

As far as I was concerned, the matter wasn't yet closed. I had a plan that would see me as the youngest in the family replacing my older brother in that room! My idea was to frighten my brother by making him think that my granddad's spirit was still hanging around it. The first night Sammy slept there, I scratched the adjoining wall of the bedrooms, trying to make just enough noise to keep him awake. Children really can be horrible to one another!

My plans were given a real boost one day when the three of us were alone in the house together. In Sammy's bedroom there was an old-fashioned wardrobe with two really heavy walnut doors. These were always kept locked since the weight of them when not secured made them creak open.

While the others were in the living room watching our new color TV, I crept into the middle room, unlocked the wardrobe doors, switched on the radio, and tiptoed quickly to the bathroom.

"Get oot ay that room, ya wee pig!" Sammy shouted.

"I'm in the bathroom," I called back in my most innocent tone.

Just then, I could hear Sammy's heavy steps coming to check up on me. This was followed by a terrifying scream of "Barney!" More footsteps. This time Sammy was joined by John. Both of them made for the front door past the bathroom where I was lying in wait. Realizing that I would be left in the house by myself, I threw open the bathroom door, screamed "Ah . . . Ah . . . Ah!" and fled with my brothers to the safety of my sister's house. I suppose I got caught up in the drama that I'd created.

If you can, imagine the fright my sister got when the three of us battered at her door demanding to be let in. "It's Barney!—a ghost!—he was coming to get us!" We blurted out all kinds of ridiculous things, hoping that she'd believe us.

"It wiz ma granddad," Sammy said.

"Ah seen um, Betty," John chipped in.

"Aye, so did ah!"

Betty turned to me, asking, "Did you huv any thin ta do way this?"

"Naw, Betty," I said. "A wiz in the toilet. Bit ah seen um as well, so ah did."

By the time we finished our complete version of what occurred, it was beginning to sound more like *The Amityville Horror.* Betty accompanied us back to the house. The front door was still wide open. After she went around and checked that everything was all right, Betty reassured us that we hadn't seen the ghost of my grandfather, but that it was all in our imaginations.

We were instructed not to tell my mum of this event, as it would upset her, and were reminded that there were no such things as ghosts. So when my mum came home from shopping, we never mentioned the ghostly episode. In fact, it was forgotten almost at once, as the contents of the shopping bags were much more interesting. "Did you get us anything in town?" we all wanted to know.

Later that evening as we were getting ready for bed, there was a reluctance on Sammy's part to enter his bedroom. I wonder why!

"Da, ah think I'll sleep in wi' thum tonight," he said.

"Whit's wrang wi' you?" Dad asked.

"Ah don't like that room," Sammy replied.

"Kin ah huv it, Da?" I chirped.

"Well, as long as somebody sleeps in it, ah don't care," my father replied.

It was done. I had it. The scheming little psychic got his way . . . eventually. And from then on in it was mine until we moved some five years later.

I now have two sons, Paul and Steven. Both show signs of having psychic abilities, although it has never occurred to me to point this out to either of them. Paul, the oldest, is 21, and studying history at the University of Glasgow.

If anything, he challenges my mediumship at every opportunity. Paul takes great pleasure in explaining to me how all my work can be put down to chance or probability. He often says things like, "Dad, if these people believe what you tell them, then good, but really, I'm surprised you actually believe that spirit entities are speaking to you." At 21, we think we know it all! But even *he* changed his mind when he came to watch me demonstrate at the university in front of the type of people he considers his peers.

Steven, who's 18, is a more sensitive and artistic young man. He has a great love for art and drama and likes to take part in all kinds of sports. Throughout his childhood, he displayed both psychic and telepathic gifts.

I remember one occasion when driving past the Hilton Hotel in Glasgow. Steven, who was only ten at the time, suddenly said, "I wonder what it's like in room 1308?" I asked him why that particular room. All Steven could say was that he "saw" the number appear in front of him when he looked at the hotel.

We gave no more thought to the matter and carried on with our previous conversation. It wasn't until a week later that I realized that Steven's vision of the number 1308 was, in fact, a premonition, for I was invited to the Hilton to give a private sitting to one of the guests . . . who happened to be staying in room 1308. Considering all the rooms in a hotel of that size, I wonder what the chance would be of guessing that.

Kate, my ex-wife, and I didn't always agree on psychic matters. But one thing we did completely agree upon was that neither of us would influence the children with our own beliefs. Both our sons are very sensitive and clever. They each display compassion in their own ways. We felt that as long as our children were cared for and felt loved and guided in their lives, they could decide for themselves which religious or spiritual paths to follow—or not, as the case may be—when they were old enough to choose.

I strongly believe that if you notice psychic abilities in your child, you shouldn't make a fuss about it. Neither should you scold them for it. Children have such fertile imaginations and can invent all sorts of fanciful episodes that it becomes difficult to know what is psychic and what is imagination.

Kids have enough to contend with as they grow up without ideas of other dimensions filling their minds. If a child truly is mediumistic, the gift will grow with age, as with any other gift, like art or music.

As a medium, life can be strange, sometimes even lonely. I, for one, hope that my children express their gifts in this world in their own individual ways.

❊   ❊

CHAPTER 16

ANIMALS IN THE SPIRIT WORLD

"Do animals go on to the spirit world?" Mediums are often asked this question. I have no doubt that they do. During my time as a medium, I've relayed evidence of animal survival to many people.

Don't get me wrong. I'm not suggesting that animals come and talk to me. I mean, I'm not some kind of Dr. Dolittle to animals in the spirit world. But more often than not, when a spirit communicator passes information to a friend or loved one, they mention their beloved pets that are with them on the Other Side.

One of the most difficult things I've had to do in recent years was take my old Labrador, Elsa, to the vet to be put to sleep. I remember thinking, *Of all people, I should be able to handle this situation. No problem!* How wrong I was. The moment I looked down at Elsa's big brown eyes, as the vet was about to administer the fatal injection, quite frankly I could feel such a lump in my throat that I thought I would choke. When I was asked if I would like to say any last words, I had never before experienced such emotion in a single moment as that one.

The feeling of responsibility is enormous. For the rest of that day I was so depressed, wondering if I'd done the correct thing. I could not help but think of Elsa's beautiful golden face staring up at me, with those deep, dark, sad puppy eyes of hers. What a terrible and traumatic day.

That evening, I was to conduct a service at Kilmarnock Spiritualist Church. The very last thing I wanted to do was stand up in public and speak to people. However, after giving the matter a lot of thought, I decided to go. Even as I sat on the platform, listening to the host announce my name, all I could think about was Elsa.

Like most other occasions when I'm about to work, the feeling of Spirit moving through me filled me with energy and inspiration. All thoughts emptied from my mind, and I was soon giving messages to people in the congregation.

The last message of the night is the only one I can remember. I was directed to a lady at the back of the large church. After she accepted the contact from the spirit world, I was suddenly aware of a dog sitting beside her. I told her about this, and she started to sob.

As the message progressed, it became clear that this lady had only recently put her dog to sleep. Here I was telling this woman that her beloved pet was fine in the spirit world, that it looked so young and full of life, and I'd just gone through the same agony of saying "Adieu" to a much-loved pet.

At the close of the message, the lady was given the news from her mother on the spirit side that she had indeed done the proper thing for the animal, as it had been suffering quite a bit of pain, much like Elsa. I took great comfort from this message. But strangest of all, the dog in question was a golden Labrador, the same as Elsa. The timing of the spirit people is really quite amazing, don't you think?

❋

It has often been said that our pets give us unconditional love. It's that vital bond of love that transcends the so-called vale of death. Why should it matter if that love is forged between two people or someone and their beloved animal? There's a lot we could learn from the animal kingdom about love. Love is instinctive, and animals do most things by instinct. Of all the pets I've been privileged to have in this life, there isn't one that I can say I loved more than the others. Each had its own personality, its own consciousness. After all, it's the consciousness that survives physical death, so why shouldn't the personalities and consciousness of sentient animals, like domestic pets, live on and indeed progress spiritually as we do?

The times that I, and so many other mediums, have given evidence to people about the continued life of their pets in the spirit world are countless. I've received hundreds of letters of thanks from grateful people saying how uplifted they felt upon hearing that their pets were in the spirit world, and to know that on certain occasions they've visited them from the Other Side.

I've seen spirit animals so many times. I've heard them and sensed them. I even had an out-of-body experience where I found myself surrounded by dogs in the spirit world, some of which I recognized. All seemed very friendly toward me. I've even been privileged enough to touch spirit animals and feel their soft, warm fur beneath my hand. What's more, to feel the love they radiate is truly something else. As with all experiences of Spirit, there can be no substitute for those you undergo yourself.

I could cite countless cases of my encounters with animals on the spirit side, and find just as much joy and satisfaction in reuniting people with their pets as with their human partners and friends. All I can add is this: If you accept that the spirits of men and women live on after death, is it so hard to imagine that animals also continue?

For I believe that once the precious life-giving spark of spirit enters into an animal—be it a much-loved cat, goldfish, hamster—whatever—nothing, not even death, can vanquish it. Spirit is indestructible, no matter what its form.

Obviously because of their close association with humans and the love given to them, domesticated animals develop their individuality and personality more than other species. But I'm totally certain that all animals, whether of feather, fur, or fin, merely move on to a higher realm when their time arrives to quit the Earthly scene. And I know, too, that when the day comes that we pass on, our much-loved pets will also be there to greet us with a wagging tail or a warm and gentle purr of sheer delight. Yes, on the Other Side, the lion truly shall lie down with the lamb.

❉   ❉

CHAPTER 17

TRANCE, GUIDES, AND TEACHINGS

Trance mediumship is probably the most evidential form of contact given from the spirit world. But the sad fact about trance communication is that not many mediums today demonstrate proper deep or controlled trance states.

Over the past 12 years, I've witnessed many mediums claiming to work in trance. Unfortunately, of those I've seen, few are actually working in this very rare state.

The idea of a medium going into trance, giving up a part of their mind and body so that the spirit control can link in a much stronger way, thus allowing a better means of communication, should create a much clearer form of contact from the Other Side.

The information coming across must surely be more precise. Any evidence, you would think, has to be more conclusive. Yet on so many occasions, spirit controls talk at great length about such diverse subjects as aliens from outer space or the origin of crop circles. Some seem to even predict the end of the world. Believe it or not, I once listened to a so-called spirit guide talking about her life as a dolphin. I ask you!

I find it difficult to believe that some can delude themselves in this fashion. Surely spirit people who have a chance to communicate in such a special way would say more about things that have a bearing on the lives of those they're speaking to rather than garbled messages about strange phenomena or ridiculous situations, such as once being a sea creature.

It's because of this type of nonsense that trance mediumship comes under such attack from the skeptics. Sadly, these "mediums" are more willing to demonstrate their charades in public than true practitioners.

Something I've come to learn about genuine mediums is this: When their gift has reached a high standard, it's more often shared only with those who really need it—and, what's more, in private.

Many of the best mediums refuse to work for churches or organizations for fear of being put into the same category as those who think they're good but are merely deluding themselves and their sitters.

Some of the most exceptional evidence I've seen, heard, or sensed came through true trance mediums. In addition, the simple teachings their communicators and guides offered were uplifting, comforting, and wise.

Another hallmark of the genuine trance medium is that there's never any fuss when the control first links with them—no moaning, groaning, or exaggerated movements of the medium's body. In fact, the whole process is simple and natural, as it should be.

For the best part of 12 years I've been fortunate to sit in a very good trance circle. None of the mediums in our circle, except myself, have demonstrated their trance abilities in public. Even I have only done so on two occasions. Yet so many people have come through the circle and have been privileged to share the experiences spirit people have imparted freely.

During our circle's early days, I came to learn about my own spirit guide and helpers. As ours was a trance circle, the object was to learn to trust Spirit by allowing communicators to overshadow us. First, through meditation, we let go of the control of our conscious mind.

The spirit people around us filled the space with their own consciousness, impressing information of their thoughts and sensations into the minds of the mediums. It's like an intense type of telepathy, which causes images and feelings to be picked up at the same time. The more you can let go, the more receptive you become to the presence of their personality and the image of the spirit being.

The discipline in our circle was patience. The idea was that each sitter would take time and forge a strong link with their spirit guide, no matter how long it took. Whenever you received spiritual impressions, they had to be tested. All information that came through was to be verified, otherwise you didn't progress. It didn't matter that I or any other in the group was clairvoyant, for we were never allowed to give messages to each other.

We had to get to know who was working with us—and if a spirit control came to speak to the group, they'd have to pass certain tests. Only when all of this was complete could you take a step forward in your development.

For the first few years, I certainly learned patience. No matter how eager I was, spirit helpers seemed to be in no rush. Each week, in my mind, I asked all sorts of questions of them, eagerly awaiting an instant answer. No chance! I'm not so stupid that I couldn't recognize a lesson in patience when it was being taught.

But every time I got to the stage of giving up, something nice would happen, like one night when, on the way to church, I decided I'd had enough of the development circle. I thought about leaving and perhaps doing something else with my time. Looking back, I suppose it was just a case of feeling a little bit down at that particular time.

However, by the time I reached the church to attend the circle, I'd completely forgotten how I was feeling, settled down in my chair as usual, and I just got on with it.

Not too long into the meditation, I became aware of someone standing directly in front of me. In my mind's eye, I could see the figure of a person dressed in what looked like a habit. The bizarre thing about this vision was that I couldn't see the form's head. Just then, the hands of the person reached out toward me, and I felt compelled to raise my hands toward theirs.

No sooner had the thought occurred to me than my hands were in motion, lifting up to join those of the figure before me. At the point where our hands touched, I was amazed to feel how real they felt. They were solid, warm, and quite coarse. The next thing I knew, I was being pulled to my feet. During all of this, I still couldn't see the figure's head.

At this point, I began to realize that I was standing outside myself. My physical body was being worked by someone else. The person, who seemed imaginary initially, now felt as solid as I did.

Working my body was a small Chinese-looking man. He appeared to be moving it by a process of thoughts. Meanwhile, the person I saw first—she was the one dressed in a habit—seemed to be speaking, yet the words were coming out of my mouth.

All of this happened in what felt like an instant when, in fact, 20 minutes or so had passed. The feelings I experienced during this episode were indescribable. To say that I felt lifted, exhilarated, or even on a high wouldn't begin to come close to what I truly felt.

At the end of the circle, everyone was anxious to know what had happened to me. Apparently, I got to my feet, walked across the room, up the stairs at the side of the platform, stood and spoke for some time on spiritual matters, then walked back to my seat and sat down.

Of course, the voice speaking wasn't recognized as my own, but that of one of the spirit people who works with me. I described the two people I was aware of and the immense feeling of upliftment.

At this point, Mrs. Primrose broke in, saying, "You were in a deep state of trance. I saw the spirit people you mentioned. They will be working with you like that for a while."

As I tried to take all of this in, she added, "Oh, yes, I was to tell you from 'them' that they heard you on the way to church tonight. This is their way of saying you're ready to move forward."

By moving forward, the spirit helpers meant that I was ready to experience working in a trance state, and for the next couple of years, I did. As the years went by, I got to know the guides and helpers working with me. There seem to be a number of them, but my main guide is the little Chinese man I saw that night. Because I can't pronounce his full name, I call him Chi.

It would appear that Chi lived quite sometime ago. As far as I'm aware, he was just a humble little man. The few times I've seen him, he's always looked the same. I've never seen him dressed in magnificent robes or anything like that. Each time he comes to work with me in trance, I feel his light, wispy beard and mustache brush against my face. Whenever Chi speaks through me, the content is always so simple yet filled with grace and wisdom.

I became so used to his presence that I suppose it never occurred to me that any other spirit person might want to use me in this manner, which is why I later got quite a shock. It happened one night when giving a private sitting to a young man, who came to see me not long after the death of his father.

When I give a private sitting to someone, it's always done with me in complete control of my faculties. By this, I mean that I never go into trance. As far as I was concerned, this was only done in our circle, but I was about to learn another lesson—don't ever make hard-and-fast rules when you work for the spirit world!

The sitting started out quite well. I made contact with the young man's father, who was relaying information on how he passed over. Then I heard him saying that his name was Jimmy. None of this was out of the norm.

Just then, I became very aware of a voice telling me to relax. The voice was coming from deep inside me. I started to feel my head go light. Even though I was still speaking to my sitter, I couldn't hear the words coming out. What happened next was strange, even for me.

I opened my eyes to see the young man sitting in front of me. His face was soaked with tears, his eyes wide, with a look of astonishment on his face.

"Are you all right?" he asked.

"Well, yes," I replied, wondering what had occurred while I was "gone." I knew I must have been in trance, but had no idea what happened.

"Would you mind telling me what went on?" I asked.

"Don't you know?" said the sitter.

The fact was that I had no idea at all! Normally when I go into trance, I have some sort of awareness, but on this occasion I was completely out of it.

According to the sitter, I was speaking to him in my normal voice about his father when he noticed that my voice began to change. Apparently, a voice speaking with a

French accent seemed to take over. What's more, the voice was that of a woman, one calling herself Dominica.

The young man went on to tell me that Dominica said she was one of my spirit helpers and that she had entranced me and made contact to prove the authenticity of her life on Earth some 500 or more years ago.

Dominica told my sitter that he'd just come back from the place where she lived all that time ago, San Sebastián, in the Basque region of Spain. This, it seemed, was true. She added that he was the last person ever to be allowed to sleep in her convent.

Again, this was true. I learned that while backpacking through Europe, my sitter wandered from his original planned route, ending up in San Sebastián, looking for somewhere to sleep for the night. The only place open to him was an old convent at the top of a mountain. It would, he was told, close the following day.

The communicator then went on to describe a part of his trip that he'd told no one. Apparently, the young man was mugged while passing through France. Since his money was stolen, he had to spend the night in the home of one of the French police officers. Dominica asked the sitter to tell me all of this so I could investigate some of the details in the future.

After all this, she gave perfect evidence of the young man's father in the spirit world. It seems that while Dominica was speaking, all the plants in the room started to shake.

But it was the young man's final words that really surprised me. "She said to tell you that she was the one who took your hands and lifted you from your seat, whatever that means." There was no possible way my sitter could have known that this incident had indeed occurred.

Dominica gave me so many things to look for about her life. It has taken me seven years to find out that she really did live back in the 15th century. Everything she said about her life was correct. She was French, but went to live in a convent in San Sebastián, where she later died as a result of her newfound beliefs. There's so much I could write about this soul, but the only person who needs to be convinced of her existence is me—and, of course, I am.

Once a spirit person gives me some kind of evidence about their Earthly identity and it's verified, I no longer question it, or, indeed, their existence. And both Chi and Dominica have passed that test.

It's very important for any medium to check information given from their spirit helpers. Even those who teach us from the Other Side encourage us to "test the spirits." After all, it's mediums who put themselves up for ridicule in the public eye. Therefore, total trust must exist between medium and guide.

As mentioned earlier, teachings we receive from spirit mentors are so simple, filled with so much common sense. The benefits of these lessons normally come to us when we need them most. I try not to ask too much of my helpers, for I've come to know and understand that when they have something to teach me, I will be told. What's for you will never go past you!

This is why I don't generally put myself up for public demonstrations of trance. People quite often ask so many selfish questions of Spirit, thinking that those in the higher realms have the answers to all their problems. Life on Earth is just not meant to be that simple, I'm afraid. We're here to learn, and often by our mistakes, too!

Another important point is that spirit communicators don't instantly become possessed of all the knowledge in the universe. Indeed, it's debatable just how far they can see ahead. Then there's the complex question of free will. We on Earth aren't puppets on a string and have our own choices to make.

Sadly, if a gift like trance mediumship is too available, some abuse it. Like all things that are precious, people by their very nature want to own it. My advice to those who seek answers through the gift of trance is this: If you feel that the trance is true and the speaker is of a higher mind, please treat the individual with the respect he or she deserves. Never be afraid to test the person, but always be courteous. Listen carefully to what you're told, remembering that the voice of Spirit would never deliberately misguide or mislead you. And remember: Be careful what you ask for—you might just get it!

Last—but certainly not least—always exercise your own judgment, intelligence, and reason. Never embark on a course of action simply because someone in the spirit world advises you to. Those on the Other Side are still very human and can make mistakes, too. No one is infallible on either side of the veil.

As a medium, I never use my contact with the spirit world as an aid in my life, although the trust I've built with my guides and helpers will, hopefully, help me assist many others.

During a trance demonstration Dominica gave in England, one lady asked, "What is the greatest problem that people have in this life?" The reply was this:

"Fear. Fear is the one major problem that humankind shares. All of our problems are born out of fear. You become afraid when you lack things, but even more afraid when you have things, fearing that you will lose what you now have. That which you fear most are death and dying.

"All of your life you are plagued by the thought of death, either your own or those whom you love. Try to accept the impermanence of the physical world in which you live. Remember that all life is in constant motion. By trying to hold on to a particular part of your life, you will become restricted and afraid of change. When first you learn not to fear, this is the first day of your true life. Let us in the Spirit teach you so that you will no longer fear, and your lives can be lived blessed with freedom and peace."

✳   ✳

CHAPTER 18

AN ATTORNEY'S
ACCOUNT

In 1996, a friend of mine, Anthony Davidson, a solicitor in Glasgow, called and asked if I would see a friend of his from America who was going to be in town for a few days. "Of course," I said. All Anthony told me was the man's name, Richard Rosin.

We met at Anthony's house on the afternoon of August 12—and it was the beginning of a friendship that continues to this day. I'll allow Richard to tell the story in his exact words:

> On August 29, 1994, the most gentle, kindly disposed young man I've ever known was brutally murdered by five cowardly predators across the street from where he peacefully resided. He was 27 years old and was a brilliant scholar. He had wanted to devote his life to teaching young people.
>
> In the normal course of events, he would have married my daughter and become my son-in-law. Some 16 months later, my beloved daughter, who was his mirror image in terms of gentility and kindness, died of a broken heart, by her own hand.
>
> She was 21 years old. She had always been a delightful and loving child. Throughout her too

short life, she brought constant joy and happiness to others, believing that if you did good in the world, it would come back to you. It always had . . . until that August day.

I have a Scottish solicitor friend, Anthony, who has a great interest and belief in Spiritualism. He suggested that I travel to Glasgow and meet with Gordon Smith. Although skeptical, I trusted Anthony's judgment and agreed to come to Glasgow.

On a sunny afternoon, August 12, 1996, Anthony picked me up at my hotel and took me to his house. Shortly thereafter, there was a knock at the door and a very pleasant-looking, smiling young man entered the room. His demeanor and affect were such that you immediately felt relaxed and comfortable in his presence. His name was Gordon Smith.

We sat by a large window. As the light came streaming in, filling the room, Gordon asked if he could put his hand on mine. Such was the beginning of a journey that's difficult to explain. Its true belief lies in experiencing it for yourself. Gordon began a conversation that he was part of, and described what he was hearing, referring to a young woman who had recently passed into the spirit world. He mentioned a connection to Canada, a continuous and repetitive reference to law, and a year that had passed with so many changes, an incredulity that so much could happen, and a blackness attached to the year.

As Gordon continued, it was obvious that he was experiencing something highly emotional. He was perspiring in a room that was cool, and talked of dizziness, his head hurting, and "loads and loads of tears."

Gordon continued that "nobody expected this," talked of a ricochet, a lady dressed in a long white outfit, and a disbelief that "she is not here." He referred to an "M" appearing above my head. This was the first initial of the first name of my dear daughter's beloved friend. Gordon said he heard the song "Wish Me Luck As You Wave Me Goodbye," as if he were witnessing my daughter as she began her own journey in departing this Earth to find and join her true love.

I had placed a picture on the table in front of us, but said nothing. Gordon indicated that this was the lady he saw in the spirit world, now safe, having been trapped for a time on the Earth plane. "I'm feeling a bright light," said Gordon. "Leaving this world there's a sense of freedom, but an anchor of pain has been left."

Gordon could not have realized how prophetically true his revelations were. The picture was of my daughter, Beck, and the pain of a parent burying a child is unlike any other. It truly is an unnatural sequence that plummets you to the lowest level of sadness imaginable.

How could any of what Gordon related be explained? Gordon knew nothing of my daughter's untimely death; that the family of Moez, her partner in life to be, lived in Canada; of the 18-month prosecution in the American courts; and of the five who so brutally took the life of gentle Moez. How could Gordon have described so accurately the effect of the year of changes that were in actuality beyond the comprehension of those to whom they occurred?

I'm an American lawyer, trained and schooled at an Ivy League university in finance and then law, two disciplines that demand a rigorous order and level of proof. What I'd heard and witnessed defied what I could explain. And yet I knew what I'd heard and seen—of this there was no doubt. The comfort I felt from the experience was unmistakable.

I returned to Glasgow the following June and met with Gordon again, only to continue this most unique and rewarding relationship. Once more, we met at Anthony's house. Gordon began to talk of a powerful source of energy he was feeling. He was being taken back three months to March, which he felt was significant. This was the month of my daughter's birthday, a fact that Gordon had no way of knowing.

Gordon began to talk in an almost soliloquy format and spoke of a seminar that I was to attend in the fall. I knew of no such seminar, and yet upon my return to the United States, after the passage of a few months, I was invited to participate in one. There was another reference to Canada, this time in the context of "Have you heard from Canada recently?" My family was very close to Moez's family in Canada, and we spoke to each other often.

Gordon continued by referring to a life completed, a choice to join a loved one in the spirit world and the ability to continue to help people in a world other than ours. Once again, this was an amazingly accurate recitation of a factual pattern that Gordon couldn't have known. And once again I felt comfort in hearing it.

For the second time in two summers, I'd participated in something that I couldn't explain. Logically, there was no way that Gordon could have been in possession of the information that he related to me. It was clearly coming from some place, and its consistent accuracy suggested that it was beyond coincidence. Had someone related experiences to me, such as I'd had with Gordon, I would have been skeptical. There was no room for skepticism. I was beginning to understand. I returned to Glasgow the next summer.

It was late in the day on July 29, 1998, when I entered Gordon's residence. We sat in a room where he often meditated. There was peaceful music in the background. Gordon's dog, Charlie, quite excited by my entrance, became very calm. Gordon put his hand on mine, sat quietly, withdrew his hand, and began to speak.

Gordon described a young man standing behind my daughter in the spirit world. He said that he felt a wonderful source of energy and that his name began with the letter "M."

Gordon then changed the subject and told me that I would be going to Florida. Once again, Gordon was correct. It wasn't possible that he could have known this. In late August, I was to speak at a national convention relating to the victims of crime. Although arrangements had been made, I hadn't discussed this with anyone after leaving the United States for Glasgow. Then there was another change of subject and Gordon told me that Beck was singing "Happy Birthday" to someone whose birthday was approaching. Beck's brother, Dan, was to be 29 the next month.

What Gordon said next was more astounding than anything he'd said since we met: "Thank you for wearing my ring—it keeps me close to you. Thank you for repairing the ring." I wear a ring that belonged to my daughter. Gordon wasn't aware of this. What Gordon was also not aware of was that just before I left for Glasgow, one of the stones fell out of the ring and was lost. This bothered me very much. As I didn't want to travel without the ring, which was very important to me, I went to a lapidary in Philadelphia, where I live, and had the missing stone matched and replaced.

I sat in utter disbelief. There was no way to explain what I'd just been told. Gordon was unaware of the significance of what he'd said. He was merely delivering a message. But it was one that abundantly demonstrated to me, beyond all doubt, that there were forces and energy levels that must be accepted and that cannot be proven in any other way than by experience.

My relationship and friendship with Gordon continued, and on June 16, 1999, I found myself back in Glasgow. My next stop was to be Antibes, in the south of France, for a European Law Society meeting. I had not as yet discussed my travel plans with Gordon. All he knew was that I would be in Glasgow for two days.

Gordon picked me up at my hotel late in the afternoon, and we returned to his flat. He started our time together in the same room as the year before, and began once again by holding my hand. This time he also touched Beck's ring. Gordon said that he could sense her presence, and it was very strong.

"Tell my dad I will be with him—Nice or Monte Carlo—that lovely coast." This didn't make sense to me at the time, as my destination was Antibes, not Nice or Monte Carlo. I'd planned to spend four days in Antibes. What I didn't know when I was in Glasgow was that I would change my plans in Antibes, leave after two days, and travel with friends to a lovely small town on the coast called Beaulieu, midway between Nice and Monte Carlo. I'd been told that something would happen that I had no idea would happen and then it _did_ happen. This is yet another level that must be accepted simply because it has occurred.

Gordon then made reference to the young gentleman in the spirit world, saying that he could still feel the pain, and mentioned a connection to his parents. Moez's parents had recently moved to London, and I was planning to visit them on my return from France. I hadn't mentioned this to Gordon either. Gordon, however, knew and communicated this to me.

When I originally called Gordon to tell him when I'd be in Glasgow, he told me that he was supposed to be demonstrating at a Spiritualist church on one of the evenings and invited me to attend.

I was delighted by this opportunity. After we finished our time together at his flat, we left for his scheduled appearance at the Eternal Christian Spiritualist Church in Glasgow.

Although we arrived a bit early, there were people outside waiting for Gordon. There was excitement in the air, and we entered the church to find every seat taken. The same excitement that I perceived outside permeated inside. Gordon was wearing a shirt in a lovely shade of blue, and the calmness and peacefulness he radiated was reinforced by his soothing tone.

The service began with song and prayer. As Gordon began to speak, all eyes were upon him. A quiet enveloped the room. People were standing at the back and along the side. The excitement had metamorphosed itself. Something very special was happening.

With each passing moment, Gordon delivered a message that had meaning to someone in the church. The looks of hope and anticipation turned to smiles and confirmation. Comfort, peace, and reassurance filled the room. Gordon continued, and the feelings grew. People would nod positively in response, say, "Yes, that's right," and accept and embrace what they heard with acquiescence. So powerful was it to observe, to be part of.

Here was a very special young man, with an extraordinary gift that he was sharing with all who had gathered to see him. This continued for over an hour. It was obvious that Gordon was tiring, and who wouldn't be? He had spent a full day at his shop, then time with me, and now, at the church, it was close to nine o'clock at night. The energy that was drained from Gordon as he delivered one meaningful message after another was considerable, and yet he unselfishly continued.

At the end of this special evening, those who had assembled were able to return to their worlds with a feeling of comfort and happiness that they didn't have when they arrived. Whether a recipient or an observer, the result was much the same. Gordon provided hope, comfort and the possibility of believing that death is not as final as it seems, that we are not as alone as we envision after the loss of a loved one, and that the spirit that is part of all of us continues after death. There is great and powerful consolation in each and every one of these concepts.

As I think about my friendship with Gordon and the meaningful effect he has on people, several thoughts occur to me. It's clear that if your mind is closed, by definition this closure precludes the acceptance and understanding of new information. By remaining open-minded to new information, we make it possible to accumulate and then learn from new experiences that we have.

It seems impossible to be able to prove by modern scientific standards what Gordon is able to convey. Yet, several centuries ago, I believe that interactions of this type were more common. And in their commonality there was greater acceptance. Science was not as capable of demanding as high a level of proof as exists today, and as a consequence, it was easier for people to trust their experiences and believe in them.

I've come to believe, through my own personal experiences, that there is much we can feel and experience that cannot be explained. Much of what we feel, if allowed, can provide tremendous *comfort in a situation that's too often devoid of comfort and filled with pain, loneliness, and sadness. I will probably never be able to explain with certitude how it is possible for Gordon to share with me what he has. And yet there's also no doubt that I know exactly what Gordon has shared with me and that it has, in fact, occurred not only in its own terms, but with repetitive clarity and accuracy. There's also no doubt as to the meaningful level of comfort and peacefulness that it has produced. Each is a very real, positive, and lasting feeling that should be encouraged rather than discouraged.*

It's my belief that if we remain open to the possibility of new experiences, then they'll occur and we'll all be the better for them. If we remain closed to their possibility, we'll guarantee their non-occurrence and fulfill a negative and empty prophecy. The choice is an individual one—I can only suggest and recommend what I myself have so clearly come to believe.

I guess that's enough of being serious for this chapter! Working constantly in such an intense area of life, you really have to learn not to get too bogged down with the emotions of others, otherwise you get washed away in the same emotional sea. After all, I'm here as a kind of emotional lifeguard.

Still, in these past 15 years, I've traveled all over the place, met some of the most interesting people you could imagine, and stayed as a guest in the most upscale establishments in this country and others. It has been a good old journey. When I read over my diaries of these years, it reminds me of climbing a mountain. Just when I think

I've reached the summit, I realize that I still have so much farther to climb.

Looking to the future, I wonder about some of the challenges that lie ahead for me. I've been blessed by God, and through my work He has blessed many others. Proving the reality of survival after death to others has become my life's work, and I'm dedicated to it. I can't say that I'll prove this to the entire world, but I'll have fun trying.

Having witnessed people's emotional hurt as much as I have, I often put the question of human suffering to the spirit world. The answer is almost the same time and again: "It is through your suffering that you grow."

Each one of us, it would seem, has a certain number of lessons to grow through in this material life. Each individual has different lessons, although sometimes similar in nature. These lessons have nothing to do with retribution or repayment for good or bad deeds done. In fact, they have more to do with the next life than this one.

The choice is ours. Whether or not we choose to take a spiritual step or not depends on how we react at critical points of our Earthly life. When you think that each major event in any of our lives is connected to one emotion or another, it would seem that the emotional part of our life is the section that keeps us most Earthbound, the needy part of us, the piece that wants to hold an identity for eternity.

To understand your spiritual nature, you must first learn to free yourself of the emotional. The spiritual part of you cannot be destroyed because it's connected to the God-force. When we lose the physical body, it's said that the consciousness goes on. It's a series of shedding skins, if you like. We become lighter with every spiritual step we take. Physical death is only one of them.

Here I go getting all holy and spiritually high-minded! Please just take my word for it that there's more to life than what we have now. For what it's worth, believe in yourself, and try to accept the lessons of life, whatever they may be.

But remember, too, that life is not merely an obstacle course set out for our development. It's a gift, one to be savored, enjoyed, and lived to the very fullest. For as it says in the "Desiderata," we are indeed children of the Universe, and children need light and laughter as well as training. I can do no better than end this chapter with the final words of that great manual for living: "Strive to be happy." Take my prayers and best wishes with you on your unique spiritual journey.

✻　✻

CHAPTER 19

MEDIUMSHIP AND THE MEDIA

Mediumship has taken me through many different areas of life, and because of it I've met so many varied and fascinating people, none more so than those who work in the media.

Since my early days as a medium, I've often found that those in the press and on TV nearly always insist on trying to report and show mediumship in action. In other words, they want me to demonstrate my gifts instantly, no matter how disruptive the surroundings or hostile the atmosphere. Of course, I don't mind demonstrating for skeptics, but those who are anti-mediumship automatically create a mental—and often somewhat hostile—"Prove-it-to-me-now" barrier, which is sometimes hard to penetrate.

From my point of view, it's a bit like trying to climb Mt. Everest in bedroom slippers. Really, all I ask is that someone put aside any preconceived notions and sit in a state of open-minded kindness and quiet expectation in the hopes that I can successfully link with their loved ones and friends beyond. It's odd, you know. No one expects a vicar or bishop, for example, to prove that God exists, but time after time, I'm put in the hot spot and asked to demonstrate the spirit world's reality in three minutes flat!

During the numerous times I've been interviewed and probed by presenters and journalists, they all ask the same kind of somewhat obvious, standard questions, such as: "When did you first discover you were a medium?" or "Can you see the spirits all the time?" I suppose that this is understandable, but it would be nice to be asked some original questions once in a while.

Happily, the media's approach toward mediumship has changed in recent years. Once journalists and the like were very cynical toward mediums and psychics, but now a more open-minded and serious approach often prevails.

Back in 1990, I gave an interview to a Scottish television program called *Icon*. It was my first experience being interviewed on TV. At first, I felt (understandably) very nervous about being seen by many viewers talking about my beliefs and understanding of Spiritualism, but once I'd been introduced to the researchers and production team, they put me at ease almost at once.

One of the assistant producers carried out a mock interview with me. Can you imagine what this was like? I wasn't even a full-fledged medium at this point and here I was being asked to speak on a TV program. I remember it so well. I asked my teacher, Mrs. Primrose, if she thought appearing on TV was a good idea. She didn't answer, but just gave me a look that years later I came to realize meant a very firm "No!"

The TV producers were eager to film the interview in the busy salon where I worked. I suppose they wanted to create the effect of an ordinary person who by day lived a normal life, cutting hair and chatting to people, but by night became involved in Spiritualism.

Truth be told, when the time came to do the interview, I felt very relaxed and at ease. The young lady hosting the program introduced herself to me, and we chatted for a while. Her name was Shareen Nanjiani, and sometimes she read the news on the *Scotland Today* program. Shareen was very pleasant, and I felt reassured . . . until we began the interview!

My memory of that program is a blur, but when I watch the video recording of it, I still cringe with embarrassment. Shareen looked very much at ease, a professional putting questions to someone who appears very wooden and whose behavior is like a man being interrogated—me! None of the questions posed during the mock session came up in the filmed version. Even worse was that the direction of the interview seemed to have changed from spiritual healing and mediumship to the occult and Satanism.

Of course, Spiritualism has nothing whatsoever to do with such subjects. Even though it is a recognized religion with churches throughout the United Kingdom and many other parts of the world, Spiritualism is so often wrongly lumped together with the more lurid, headline-grabbing aspects of the occult. Just remember, too, that we have our own ministers who, like Orthodox clerics, undergo a long period of training.

I felt absolutely shattered at the end of the interview and just wished it had never happened. Yet I was sure that the spirit world would have backed me on this. I was so positive about my feelings before it had begun. How could I have misread the situation so badly? My thoughts were all over the place. One thing was firm in my mind—I would never go on television again!

One of my greatest fears at the time was that I would have to face Mrs. Primrose. I remembered the way she'd looked at me when I first told her about the program.

"Well, how did it go, son?" she asked me.

"It was fine," I said a little hesitantly, and probably not very convincingly.

Mrs. Primrose took me by the arm and walked me into the church office. "Now," she added, "tell me how you really feel—and be honest."

I began to tell her how awful the whole thing had been, and that I felt I'd been tricked by the change of approach and the line of questions.

Mrs. Primrose just looked at me again, only this time she smiled and began to explain how she knew that it would be a disaster, but as a developing medium I had to learn to deal with such situations.

"I had to allow you to go through this lesson," she explained. "It's just as well it happened so early in your development."

The only thing I could say was, "I will never do anything like that again!"

"Is that so?" Mrs. Primrose replied somewhat quizzically, and then added, "I think that you will, only next time you will have learned a very valuable lesson indeed, one that will hold you in good stead for the future."

I wondered what she could have meant. Would I really go back on television at some time? I was sure that I would not. In fact, it would have been the last thing I would have thought about doing.

Just as I turned to leave the little office, my old teacher looked at me very sincerely. "Gordon," she said, with a slight smile, "just remember this: Not all things that Spirit teaches us are pleasant. In fact, most are not, but they were right there with you all the way and will be when you do it again. Just learn to trust them. Oh—and one more thing: You never let them down, just yourself."

When I left Mrs. Primrose's church that night, I wondered what she meant when she said I'd be doing TV again. It had been a terrible experience for me, one I felt sure I didn't want to experience again. As always, my teacher was correct, for it wasn't too much longer before the world of television came knocking on my door again.

So often I say, "There's no such thing as coincidence!"—and so many times I'm right. One day in September 1999, one of the staff members in our salon was ill and couldn't come to work. It was to be my day off, but at the last minute I received a call at home asking if I could come to work. As I had no other plans for the day, I agreed.

An hour or so after arriving at work, a young man stopped to peer into the salon's window. It looked as if he was unsure as to whether or not to come inside. The man seemed a little bit lost when finally he pushed open the door and asked if he could have his hair cut. One of the barbers told him he could, so he sat down in the chair next to mine, and my colleague asked how he would like his hair styled.

So close are the chairs in the salon that conversations can be heard in all quarters. The young man began to chat about his work. He told the other barber how he worked for the BBC and was researching a program where they hoped to feature the medium Gordon Smith. My ears pricked up at that moment, but I said nothing. Instead, I winked to my colleague, who understood at once that I wanted to hear more before volunteering any information.

The chap from the BBC carried on talking about the nature of his forthcoming program, and how he hoped that the medium would take part in the filming of some of the most haunted places in Edinburgh. Then he complained that it had been so difficult trying to find this man, Gordon Smith, and had been told he might be demonstrating his mediumship at the University of Glasgow in the near future. At this point, I could no longer resist the chance to have some fun.

"Oh, that happened two days ago, sir," I said. The customer turned to me. "I heard that he wasn't very good," I added. "In fact, I believe he makes it all up."

This brought an immediate response from the BBC man. "I've heard differently," he volunteered. "Gordon Smith seems to have gained some respect among the Spiritualist community. You see, it was the people at the Spiritualist church who recommended him for our program."

My colleague began to smile, as did I. Eventually, I confessed to being the elusive medium. At first, he didn't believe me, thinking that the whole thing was a setup, but after the other barbers and some more regular customers backed up my claims, he eventually accepted this.

What was more difficult for him to take in was that he had no real intention of coming in to this particular salon. It came out that the BBC man had decided to go into the first barber's shop on his route, which happened to be Byres Road. I should explain that my salon is the first of several on that particular route. After he'd recovered from the shock of this coincidence, we talked about the program that he was putting together and what he wanted me to do.

The plan was to film some of the (allegedly) most haunted places in the city of Edinburgh. Using both psychic researchers and the talents of a respected medium, it was hoped to catch a glimpse of a ghost on camera or maybe gain some insight into the nature of the so-called hauntings.

After much thought on my part, which included a short mental consultation with my spirit friends, I agreed to take part in the program. The filming was scheduled for that November. I found myself with Daphne, a psychic researcher, and a fellow named John—someone who was skeptical on the subject—being chauffeured to Scotland's capital to dredge up the past and maybe shed some light on the once-plagued streets of Edinburgh.

Upon our arrival at the entrance to one of the old dungeons that ran beneath the city, the film crew, production team, and Fred McCauley, the program's host, greeted us. Mr. McCauley hosts various television and radio shows in Scotland.

Fred, it seemed, was being briefed on the history of the old streets by one of the city's tour guides, a young Edinburgh chap dressed in a top hat and long black cape. Once all the cameras and lights were in place and Fred had gone over his script, filming began.

At first I just stood around and watched. I couldn't really say that I was sensing anything other than the damp smell and the sound of water running down the old stone walls. Daphne, however, appeared to be doing much better with a meter that registered moisture. Meanwhile, skeptic John was giving his interview to Fred about how it was all just a load of rubbish and such. The only person in the old dungeon to display any enthusiasm was the tour guide. While carrying a tall church candle and swishing his long black cape for effect, he described in full detail how visitors on his tours were often scared half to death by the screams and touches of the many troubled ghosts and phantoms said to haunt these tunnels.

Several hours came and went—and still no sight of a ghost or even a sniff of one! Eventually, we arrived at Mary Kings Close (a "close" in Glasgow is a narrow road), which is said to be the most haunted of all the streets. We were all tired by now and everyone's cynicism was more than apparent. It must have been at the very moment my mind was drowning in boredom that I began to tune in to the spirit world. Even though I wasn't present to give messages from the Other Side, somehow I lapsed into a sort of daydream.

I remember vaguely hearing all of the assembled ghost-busters muttering about how the energies in the close were very different from all the other dungeons and tunnels, when into my mind came the voice of an elderly man. He was repeating a single word over and over again. This became so loud inside my head until I eventually said the word out loud while staring straight at Fred.

His mouth fell open as I began to repeat word for word all that was now coming through my mind. Everyone in the dank old room fell silent, listening to this great diatribe that I was spouting in Fred McCauley's direction. All I can tell you is that it was Fred's old granddad, coming to give him a message of comfort from the spirit world.

After what seemed like an hour and yet could have been no more than five minutes, Fred finally said something. "I want that tape!" he demanded. That was all he said. Fred didn't want the BBC to use this footage in the program and appeared quite shaken by the whole business.

I spent some time chatting to him on his own away from everyone else so that I could explain just what had occurred. Once it had all sunk in, Fred then explained the relevance of what it meant to him. Like most people who have never had a personal message from the spirit world, he had so many questions to ask. The producer told me that he would try to persuade Fred to allow him to use the footage in the program, as he'd captured a great piece of film for television. On the other hand, I felt that Fred was well within his rights to keep what was a personal message about his family from TV and well away from the prying eyes of the public.

After the program went out, all the Scottish newspapers featured stories about what had happened in Mary Kings Close, and that the medium Gordon Smith had stunned TV presenter Fred McCauley with a message from "beyond the grave." Fred gave some interviews saying much the same thing. When the series was shown, the part that featured the "ghost hunt" in Edinburgh's most haunted places was more comical than frightening or even informative. I suppose that with people taking part with names such as Fred and Daphne, it appeared more like an episode of *Scooby-Doo.*

Still, I was undecided whether or not mediumship belonged on television, but after all the press and media interest that surrounded the Fred McCauley program, I was invited to take part in numerous talk shows and documentaries. Some, I decided, weren't for me, yet there were others that I felt wouldn't be damaging to my mediumship. As with all the things I do as a medium, I always tune in and ask the spirit world first. If the feelings that come back feel negative in any way, then I decline.

One program that I felt would be positive was the BBC's respected *Heaven & Earth* show, which goes out on Sunday mornings, and deals with current affairs and religious matters. It was around the autumn of 2000. People were still talking about the new millennium and the Age of Aquarius when filming began on a segment of the show that would feature me answering questions on mediumship and psychic matters.

"What harm can there be in that?" I asked myself. The director insisted on filming me cutting the presenter's hair while answering his questions and describing my journey as a medium. After this interview, I was to be filmed giving a more in-depth description of Spiritualism in one of the Spiritualist churches in Glasgow. Again, what harm could there be in this? Nothing, apparently, except that a voice in my head kept telling me that the film crew was up to something.

"You aren't going to film anything in a cemetery, are you?" I asked.

"Absolutely, not!" was the reply.

"Are you certain that you don't have a plan for me to give a private sitting to someone?" I questioned.

"No, Gordon, just an interview in the church," the director explained.

After we arrived and set things up in the church, the interview began. Presenter John Mahoney asked the usual kind of questions I'd come to expect, such as "Is Spiritualism a religion?" and "Do many people attend the services?"

As I started to answer, I became aware of a spirit person standing at my side. I said nothing and didn't make anyone else aware of my feelings, but just kept answering the questions. Then John asked if I could connect to the Other Side for him. At this point, the director was insisting that I try to do so. It felt like I was being goaded into performing for them.

I tried to hold back the spirit person I could feel getting stronger when all of a sudden, I spontaneously burst out with the name and address of my spirit communicator. This was much to the astonishment of one of the lighting men, who almost let go of the large light he was holding above a camera. There was no stopping me now! The director was calling out for a response from the man in question, but he just stood there looking at me in much the same way that Fred had done almost a year before.

As the message poured out and the information became more and more specific, the spirit contact became very emotional, so much so that I called a halt to the whole proceedings so that I might continue in private with the unsuspecting member of the film crew.

The feature went out as part of *Heaven & Earth* some weeks later . . . without the segment with the message for the lighting man. Once again, I had given a very accurate and in-depth message from a loved one in the spirit world, yet it wasn't allowed to be shown on television. In a sense, I was somewhat disappointed, yet again I had to agree that the message was personal and relevant only to the recipient, and not really for the eyes and ears of the viewing public.

I regard mediumship messages as personal and confidential unless they're given at a public demonstration of clairvoyance. Even then, I always take care not to cause someone embarrassment or breach a confidentiality. I believe that like doctors and priests, what is said to a medium should not be broadcast—in this case, literally—to others.

A part of the film featured a clip of the BBC presenter standing in a graveyard asking the question, "Will Gordon have a message for me?" So much for the promise not to do so. Other than that, the program went fine. The rest of the short film showed an interview in the salon. After this segment, the film shot back to the studio, where the assembled guests discussed the subject of mediumship among themselves.

I was very pleased that the episode with the lighting man was mentioned, even if they couldn't show it. What's more, the host commented, "When I watched Gordon give that message, I was left with two options. One is that he's a very good fake, or that he's a truly gifted medium. I prefer to go with the second option." Somehow, I think that from the spirit world Mrs. Primrose would—or rather will—have approved of the *Heaven & Earth* venture!

Even so, looking back over these events, it would appear to me that the world of television wasn't really ready for mediumship yet. On the occasions when I was able to give accurate evidence to a recipient, the footage still couldn't be shown.

It's the same old problem that mediums have faced for many years when asked to work in this way. The moment that TV producers surround mediums with people and ask them to tune in to just one person, you simply can't guarantee that it will be successful. After all, mediums can't call up particular spirit beings, and what's more, shouldn't do so on demand. Spirit return is entirely voluntary. Mediums can't call up the so-called dead. Each and every sitting or attempt at spirit contact should be regarded as an experiment in two-world communication, as we're dealing with very subtle forces. It's just like tuning in a radio. Unless the wavelength is exactly right, you get interference—or the wrong station altogether!

For all these reasons, I decided not to be filmed doing my work on television again unless producers could assure me that my mediumship would be shown in a surrounding that's natural to me and not something solely set up for the sake of a program. The medium of television may well turn out to be a part of the future for mediumship . . . but if that's so, I'm certain that the spirit world will have a big part in this.

✳ ✳

CHAPTER 20

THE ITALIAN CONNECTION

O f all the places I've served as a medium, there's none more rewarding than the beautiful spiritual center in the north of Italy called Cassia del Albero. Using mediumship and spiritual healing, it was established some years ago with the aim of helping people who have lost loved ones. Throughout the year, there are courses on how to develop and understand both healing and mediumship, as well as demonstrations of clairvoyance and private sittings.

The English medium Sue Rowlands introduced me to the center, called Casa del Albero. Sue is a very well-respected medium in the United Kingdom and in other countries around the world, and it's due to her mediumship that several centers like this one have been founded. Sue's hard work over many years has brought much comfort and healing to grieving people in all walks of life. I've worked with Sue many times and admire her no-nonsense approach, knowing full well that she's a very compassionate person and that this work means a lot to her.

The first time I worked with Sue in Italy was in the year 2000. Having heard so much about it, I couldn't wait to reach the center. Carla, the lady who founded it, suffered so badly after the death of her young son that she went to a demonstration of mediumship that Sue gave in Italy some years earlier. Sue was able to bring a great change into Carla's life by making contact with her son in the spirit world. Through her beautiful center, Carla now offers grieving parents the chance to be helped in the same way.

The doors of this center are also open to sick children from all over the world who require healing—and all of this arose from just one spirit message from a son to his desperate mother.

After arriving by plane in Bologna, we were taken by car 30 or so miles north to a little town called Fossili, where the Casa del Albero lies in the middle of flat countryside. It's all so very different from the rugged hills and mountains that I love so much in my native Scotland. The building is a refurbished farm-type property that looks like so many we saw on our journey from the airport.

Once we got settled into our rooms, Sue introduced me to some of the people she's come to know well in her time working there, especially those who would become our right arms. By this, I mean our translators Christina, Manuela, and Monica. These three very pleasant and friendly women all have an interest in the work that mediums do. They were extremely professional and realized the importance of translation when interpreting for a medium. When you think about it, a simple word can make a massive difference in what you're trying to convey in just one sentence—let alone what might be a fairly lengthy spirit message. I suppose you could say that translation is a form of mediumship in itself, as it involves being given information from one source but trying not to lose the essence of what's being conveyed.

During our seminar, Sue and I gave talks, workshops, and demonstrations of clairvoyance, as well as many private sittings for those Carla felt required help. Working for people who respect both you and what you do really does make such a huge difference. Probably because of its staunch Roman Catholic background and culture, Italy has few mediums of its own. When demonstrating somewhere like that, so many people turn out to see what it's all about, along with those who need reassurance about life after death and the hope of contacting loved ones.

Of all of the work that we did in the Casa del Albero, the most fulfilling related to the private sittings. The greatest reward for any true medium is to see someone who has a real need—a person who is at the end of the road, stricken with grief. To be able to turn that around and experience the change in that soul because of the work you've done is worth so much more than any financial gain.

Most of the people who have private sittings at this lovely center come because they have that genuine need for mediumship, and not simply to obtain psychic predictions. In any event, a medium's main role is to prove survival after death, not to forecast what the future may bring or give advice on a difficult problem, although spirit guidance is sometimes given.

I was especially struck by one particular sitting and can't imagine that I'll ever forget it. Monica, my translator, and I walked into the small chapel at the back of the main building where I was to give my private sittings that day. Sitting waiting for us were two people who I would guess were in their mid-40s. It was a husband and wife. In Italy, a couple will very often arrive together to see a medium. But on this occasion, I didn't have to be a medium to know that they'd lost a child and were seeking reassurance that somehow, somewhere, he still survived.

After Monica introduced us and we were all seated, I began to tune in. It was very apparent that the husband didn't wish to be there at all. His wife kept nagging at him to sit still and just listen. I don't speak Italian, but that sort of thing is the same in any language.

My translator sat patiently, waiting for me to speak. Then I looked at Monica and told her that a young man had come close to me from the spirit world. Everything that I say is kept on tape for sitters, so I always try to be as deliberate as possible when working through a translator.

"There's a young man here," I said, "who died around the age of 18 . . . ," Monica translated. Immediately, the lady began to cry. Her husband folded his arms, put his chin down on his chest, and looked even more disinterested than before. The woman spoke to him in a very agitated way. He simply nodded his head for a moment and then went back to his former position.

As the sitting continued, the lady became more and more involved. She moved to the front of her chair and was almost leaning on top of me, just inches away. Whenever I said something that directly related to her son in the spirit world, she clasped her hands together in front of her face and looked heavenward.

Even though I described the young man's looks, how he was very athletic, and that he died after having an accident on his motorcycle, his father was still unmoved. Monica was completely unaffected by the man's lack of emotions throughout the sitting, as she had often commented to me that Italian men tend to be undemonstrative in these situations.

Looking at both parents, I could see a woman whose face was wet with tears. Her body language was begging to be told more about their dear son, whom it was plain to see they loved and missed so very much. On the surface, her husband was trying to keep himself together, attempting to give nothing away to this medium who was supposed to have answers to his family's deepest pain.

I paused for a moment and asked a question in my mind to the young spirit communicator. *Please*, I said mentally, *will you tell me something that will make your father feel good?* His reply was immediate.

I began to address the father directly, even although he avoided my gaze. "His name," I said, "is Roberto." Both parents screamed out the name simultaneously. At last, now I had the attention of both of them.

I carried on by telling Roberto's father that his son wanted me to say thanks for what he had done at the football stadium in his memory. The messages came through so thick and fast by now that Monica was finding it difficult to keep up with me.

At one point they both laughed when their son told them it was time to share the same bed again. At first, his mother looked horrified, but when her husband roared with laughter, she gave way and joined him, whispering private words in his ear.

By now, both were smiling broadly and explaining to Monica that since their son's death they had slept in separate beds, and that only that morning they'd decided to put an end to this. Let me explain that while "dead" loved ones are often around our homes and places of work, they never intrude upon private occasions. Often, though, they mention everyday events to prove their spiritual proximity.

It was a truly successful sitting. As always, I felt privileged and humbled to have acted as a medium between the two worlds, to part the so-called veil and reunite loved ones. To witness the complete turnaround of two people whose faces looked strained and whose eyes showed no signs of life, but then to experience these same souls ignite with life and become completely animated was like watching a miracle take place. Even more pleasing was the way that Roberto's father strutted around the dining area of

Casa del Albero, telling anyone and everyone who would listen his joyous news. I had to ask Monica to translate for me. Apparently, he was saying, "My boy knew what I did for him, and he's happy."

✳

Just about all mediums would agree that they don't remember every message they've given. Some stick in your mind because they've been so touching or uplifting to the recipient, while others are just shocking. Keeping this in mind, I'll tell you about a message that was given during one of the sessions in Italy. All I've changed are the names that were mentioned. I think you'll see why.

It was the last day of a very busy week. "Just two more sittings to go," I said to Monica with a degree of relief. No matter how much we enjoy our work, even if it's brought upliftment and joy to many people, a medium's energy begins to deplete like anyone else who has worked non-stop for an entire week. In reality, it becomes more difficult to concentrate and tune in. Even the translators begin to flag in the latter stages. Their minds tire of thinking in two different languages, and sometimes there are difficulties in translating certain phrases or terms without losing the essence.

Monica and I sat down in our room waiting for the next sitter, who we thought was to be a lady, when in walked a tall, good-looking man in his early 30s. Dressed immaculately in designer trousers and an open-necked shirt, he never looked in my direction at all, but instead addressed my translator in Italian, then proceeded to sit down.

Monica explained to me that the sitting was booked in someone else's name, but this gentleman had decided to come along instead. The reason he spoke to Monica was twofold. One is that he claimed he couldn't speak English. The other is that mediums are never allowed to see the names or any other details of a sitter before or after a sitting.

Once this had all been attended to, we got under way. The first person to communicate was a female spirit being who told me her name was Franca. She said she was the man's aunt, adding that she had died naturally. When this information was translated to the sitter, he responded by asking whether I was quite certain about what she said.

"She assures me she died naturally," I replied, continuing by talking about the spirit lady's life, and how she pointed out to me that she had lived and died in Switzerland. This he accepted.

More information came through about the woman's life, and the sitter understood all of it. But something in my gut told me that I wasn't answering the questions the man had come in with.

A second communicator came through, saying he was this man's father. Monica began to translate. When I gave the name of Mario Bonette, both my translator's and the gentleman's mouths fell open at the same time.

No one spoke except for me. "He tells me," I said, "that you've taken over the family business and have done well so far, but this new contract isn't worth bothering about."

Mario then went on to describe a beautiful mountaintop village in Sicily where he'd lived for most of his life, as well as giving more instructions to his son on certain business deals in the future.

Just before the translation began, I instructed Monica not to bother, as I was told from the Other Side that the sitter had misled us and actually spoke perfect English. The sitting ended with my asking the man if he had any further questions. He wanted to know if I had prior access to information on those who were scheduled for sittings.

Monica jumped to her feet and defended all the mediums who worked at the center. This man had only to look at the name in which he had booked—that of a woman— which had no other information accompanying it.

I might be able to hear and see people in the spirit world, but there are times when I really can't see the forest for the trees in an Earthly sense! Only after the chat at the end of the sitting did I have any understanding of whom I was speaking to. This was especially so when he asked me if his father meant that there was no need to carry out the contract on the people who were close to his Aunt Franca when she died.

Try to imagine the horror I then felt when I realized that his father wasn't describing a family business as such, and that the contracts involved doing away with people! Still, all's well that ends well, and our young businessman went away with a whole new intention—I hope!

Going home on the plane, Sue and I shared some stories of the week, and when I told her about this particular sitting, she just laughed, saying, "Really! Nothing will ever shock me about this place. I've heard it all before." Apparently, she had encountered many such people over the years working in Italy. Mediums come across so many strange situations on their travels. Even though some are really weird, there are still more that turn out to be magnifico.

People often insist, "Gordon, it must be so exciting traveling around the world." It is—to a point. What they forget are the delays at airports, living out of a suitcase, the hours spent at 30,000 feet as a plane drones on, and the sheer amount of time involved in getting from home to a destination abroad. Believe me, there's nothing very exotic about being told that your plane will be delayed for another hour or waiting at the carousel for what seems like ages for luggage to emerge, then lining up at customs or passport control.

Yet at the end of the day, I thank God for my mediumship. Don't get me wrong—I really am just an average, normal guy, but one with a psychic gift. I regard my mediumship as both sacred and spiritual, something not to be used for personal gain, but solely to help others.

Many of my sitters are bereaved—they've lost a loved one or perhaps a dear pet that provided them with years of love, loyalty, devotion, and companionship. Yes, we can all express sorrow to a friend when someone special to them passes on, but it's impossible to know exactly how that person feels, and the depth of their sorrow and anguish. My role is not to convert anyone, but to say, "This is what I believe. Test the evidence and reach your own conclusion."

I have an unshakable belief in survival after death and the spirit world. To me, it's as real and tangible as this one. No one can take that away from me, no matter what they say or do, and no matter how harsh or hurtful the criticism may be.

I can't provide any guarantee that we're immortal beings temporarily on Earth. But if nothing else, what I can offer is the hope of survival after death. While this forms a cornerstone in all of the world's religions, Spiritualism is the only religion to offer evidence that once the physical form is stilled and at peace, we retain our memories, personalities, intelligence, and individuality after we pass on. Another central part of this gigantic jigsaw is that spirit return is both possible under the right conditions, and that it's acceptable to gain evidence of continued existence after our Earthly adventure draws to a close.

The spirit world really is one of endless possibilities—a place where the aged regain their youth; the sick and infirm, whether in mind or body, are whole once again; and where reunions occur with all who are dear to us. Love is at the very core of anything to do with Spirit. It's because of links of love that so-called dead family members and friends return to those left on Earth. It's a golden guiding force, a magical, magnetic link between here and hereafter.

I'm not a preacher—far from it! I rarely—if ever—quote from the Bible, yet its three simple words: "Love one another" neatly sum up just part of my personal philosophy of life and death. If we can find love in everything we do and say, our personal worlds and the world at large can be truly transformed.

❋ ❋

ABOUT THE AUTHOR

Gordon Smith is an astoundingly accurate medium who's renowned for his ability to give exact names of people, places, and even streets. The seventh son of a seventh son, Gordon travels all around the world demonstrating his abilities, offering healing and comfort to thousands of people. At the end of his journeys, he returns to his native Glasgow where he runs a barber shop. As Gordon says, there's nothing like a short back and sides for keeping his feet firmly on the ground! His extraordinary skills have attracted the attention of university scientists researching psychic phenomena, and countless numbers of journalists and documentary producers.

✳   ✳

❄ ❄

We hope you enjoyed this Hay House book.
If you would like to receive a free catalog
featuring additional Hay House books and products,
or if you would like information about the
Hay Foundation, please contact:

Hay House, Inc.
P.O. Box 5100
Carlsbad, CA 92018-5100

(760) 431-7695 or **(800) 654-5126**
(760) 431-6948 (fax) or **(800) 650-5115 (fax)**
www.hayhouse.com

❄

Published and distributed in Australia by:
Hay House Australia, Ltd. • 18/36 Ralph St.
Alexandria NSW 2015 • *Phone:* 612-9669-4299
Fax: 612-9669-4144 • www.hayhouse.com.au

Published and distributed in the United Kingdom by:
Hay House UK, Ltd. • Unit 62, Canalot Studios
222 Kensal Rd., London W10 5BN • *Phone:* 44-20-8962-1230
Fax: 44-20-8962-1239 • www.hayhouse.co.uk

Published and distributed in the Republic of South Africa by:
Hay House SA (Pty), Ltd., P.O. Box 990, Witkoppen 2068
Phone/Fax: 2711-7012233 • orders@psdprom.co.za

Distributed in Canada by: Raincoast
9050 Shaughnessy St., Vancouver, B.C. V6P 6E5
Phone: (604) 323-7100 • *Fax:* (604) 323-2600

❄ ❄